KU-012-703

the essence of
BUDDHISM

JO DURDEN SMITH

ARCTURUS

CITY AND COUNTY OF SWANSEA LIBRARIES	
6000291121	
Askews & Holts	21-Feb-2017
294.34	£7.99
BR	

ARCTURUS

This edition published in 2016 by Arcturus Publishing Limited
26/27 Bickels Yard, 151–153 Bermondsey Street,
London SE1 3HA

Copyright © Arcturus Holdings Limited

All rights reserved. No part of this publication may be reproduced, stored in a retrieval system, or transmitted, in any form or by any means, electronic, mechanical, photocopying, recording or otherwise, without prior written permission in accordance with the provisions of the Copyright Act 1956 (as amended). Any person or persons who do any unauthorised act in relation to this publication may be liable to criminal prosecution and civil claims for damages.

ISBN: 978-1-84193-447-1
AD000172UK

Printed in Malaysia

the essence of
BUDDHISM

WITHDRAWN
SWANSEA LIBRARIES
6000291121

Contents

Introduction

Buddhism is not a religion in the sense in which the term is commonly understood in the West. Buddhists are indeed the followers of the Buddha and of his teachings, but not in the same way that Christians are said to be the followers of Christ. The Buddha did not begin to see himself, and is not seen by Buddhists, as a God; nor did he offer his disciples any sort of path to God. No claims were made by him to any unalterable truth, nor did he demand that his teachings should simply be accepted, taken on trust or acquired through an act of faith. Instead he encouraged those who wished to make the spiritual journey he himself had undertaken to experiment for themselves as individuals, retaining what was useful to them and abandoning what was not. As he is reported to have said some 2,500 years ago to the Kalamas people in north-east India (what is now Nepal):

> Don't be satisfied with hearsay or tradition or legend, or with what's come down from your scriptures, or with conjecture or logical inference or weighing evidence or a particular liking for a view . . . or with the thought: 'The monk is our teacher'. When you know in yourselves:

'These ideas are unprofitable . . . being adopted and put
into effect they lead to harm and suffering', then abandon
them. [But] when you know in yourselves: 'These things
are profitable . . .' then you should practise and abide in
them.

The goal announced by the Buddha, in other words, might be one and
the same – the experience and understanding of ultimate truth – but
each man, woman and child is enjoined to follow his or her own path
there. This necessarily entails a tolerance of others, however different
their methods and conclusions may be. What binds Buddhists
together into one community, or *Sangha*, is this mutual tolerance,
which is sometimes called spiritual friendship. From its beginnings
until the present day, the Buddhist *Sangha* – the word originally meant
a community of monks – has remained notably free from the violent
schisms and sectarian battles, as well as witch-hunting and the rooting
out of heresies, that have been so much a part of Western religious
history.

The second thing that binds Buddhists together is respect for
the Buddha and for the trajectory of the journey that he himself took
towards spiritual truth. This involved, as we shall see, a prolonged and
directed conscious effort. Because his teachings reflect this journey,
they are much less concerned with belief than with behaviour: how to
live; how to cultivate virtue and avoid vice; and, above all, how to
unlock, through meditation, the wisdom and compassion that lies
within us all. His precepts and example, in this context, represent
both a guide-book to the the paths that should be followed and a
primer in how to arrive at the truth without the mediation of either
faith or dogma. Religious experience can be apprehended directly, so
the teaching goes, as long as – like the Buddha – the individual is

prepared to undergo a spiritual transformation and to direct his gaze within himself rather than outside into the transient material world.

The third element that unites Buddhists is expressed by the word *Dharma* (in Sanskrit) or *Dhamma* (in Pali). *Dharma* or *Dhamma* is a complex carpet of a word in which the skeins of the words 'truth,' 'teaching' and 'law' can all be found. Within its two pregnant syllables, therefore, can be found the information that the Buddha's teachings point the way to the truth and that the truth is part of a natural law which is applicable to all human beings, wherever they may be. Practising the *Dharma*, in fact, is precisely what brings us together as brothers and sisters into one *Sangha*.

The concepts of Buddha, *Dharma* and *Sangha*, known as The Three Jewels, are the three cornerstones of the Buddhist's beliefs and are the most valuable possessions in his or her spiritual armoury. A formal, ceremonial commitment is made to all three whenever an individual decides to follow the path of Buddha, as expressed in a compilation of his teachings, the *Dhammapada*:

> Not to do evil
> To cultivate good
> To purify one's mind.

By making this commitment to The Three Jewels, each new Buddhist is in effect formally renouncing the three main enemies (sometimes known as the three poisons) that stand in the way of his or her path to enlightenment: greed (desire); hatred (disgust); and ignorance (delusion). He or she is also announcing that from now on Buddha, *Dharma* and *Sangha* will be a refuge within which safety and the possibility of personal growth can be found: in fact, the Three Jewels are also known as The Three Refuges. It is, then, precisely by repeating the following formula three times that one finally declares oneself to be a Buddhist.

> I go for refuge to the Buddha
> I go for refuge to the Dharma
> I go for refuge to the Sangha

After that – after 'going for refuge' – a Buddhist can then, like the Buddha himself who left his family's palace in search of wisdom two and a half millennia ago, 'go forth' and finally become a seeker, a journeyer towards truth.

Chapter One:

The Historical Background

According to tradition, the man who was to become the Buddha – the name means 'awakened' or 'enlightened' one – was born in about 560 BC in a place called Lumbini, which was situated on the northern edge of the plain of the River Ganges, just below the Himalayas, in what is now Nepal. He was given the name Siddhartha and the clan-name Gautama ('descended from the sage Gotama') and he inherited considerable privilege. His father Suddhodana was a leader (or *rajah*) of the Shakyas, one of a number of independent peoples who occupied this corner of north-east India. Like his father, therefore, the Buddha was born a member of the immutable *kshatriya* caste of aristocrats and warriors. It is worth examining for a moment the religious and social legacy he inherited.

About a thousand years before the Buddha's birth, a race of nomadic herders, commonly known as Aryans, had migrated into northwest India from the central Asian steppe and there they had encountered the last remains of a civilization that had once rivalled the Egypt of the Pharaohs: the so-called Indus River Civilization, which seems to have been egalitarian and matriarchal and to have practised an early form of Hinduism. (The word *Hindu* derives from the Persian name for the river.) The pipal tree (*ficus religiosa*) was apparently an object of veneration, asceticism and ritual cleansing appeared to be important and the figures of a mother goddess and a male god, surrounded by animals – perhaps an early manifestation of the Hindu god Shiva – have also been found.

The Aryans, who spoke an early form of Sanskrit, gradually spread out from the Indus Valley (what is now Pakistan) into the rest of the subcontinent, carrying with them a system of beliefs and social structures that were variously imposed, rejected, modified and adapted to produce the multiplicity of beliefs and practices of later Hinduism and the ordering of Indian society. These were in fact closely interrelated from the beginning of what is now known as the Vedic Age (c. 1500–500 BC) for the Aryans brought with them a rigid and hierarchical form of society (*varna*), in which different classes were divided from each other according to their level of ritual purity. Sacrifice was absolutely central to the religious life of the period, yet the necessary rituals could only be undertaken by a priest of the highest class, the hereditary brahmin priesthood, which jealously guarded its secrets.

The Caste System

From this core developed the caste system (*jati*) that still survives in modern India and which, in its earliest and most basic form, was divided into *brahmana* (the brahmin priesthood), *kshatriya* (warriors and aristocrats), *vaishya* (traders and other professionals) and *shudra* (aboriginal cultivators and farmers). Once a person was born into one of these castes, there was – and still is – no way of leaving it. Upward mobility was simply not an option: the whole system was underpinned by that familiar word *Dharma*, which in this context meant universal law, duty to family and fealty to the system, both religious and social – in other words, knowing one's place and harmoniously occupying it. If an individual lived his life meticulously according to this sense of *Dharma*, then he might be rewarded with reincarnation into a higher caste. But this was his only chance of improvement.

By maintaining this system the brahmin priesthood displayed an element of self-interest, because it made the other castes dependent upon them for their spiritual welfare. This system of control was further reinforced by the language of the Vedas; religious texts of enormous antiquity which were passed down orally through generations of the priesthood until they were finally written down in a form of Sanskrit that had become familiar to them.

The Vedas – the word *Veda* means knowledge – gave their name (retrospectively) to the Vedic Age. There are four Vedas in all, three of which are concerned with sacrificial formulae, the rules governing the conduct of religious services and spells. The oldest of them, the Rig Veda – which is believed to go back, at least in part, to the thirteenth century BC or beyond – is a collection of more than a thousand poetic hymns. Some of these are addressed to nature gods and goddesses, but some represent profound meditations on the origin of the world and the nature of the Supreme Being or Ultimate Reality: Brahman.

Brahman was one and indivisible, all-pervading and formless, a mystery at the heart of the universe: it later came to be regarded as identical with the limitless and indefinable mystery that lay at the heart of every human being. In this context Brahman was called *Atman*, but all of its aspects were really one and the same. The divine, that is to say, was perceived as being both universal and immanent – it was within us all while we were within it. Soma, an intoxicant, seems to have been often used in Aryan religious rituals in order that the

13

celebrant could experience the continuity of Brahman and *Atman* directly, through an altered state of consciousness.

Alongside the brahminic control of the Aryan community's spiritual welfare – as made manifest in the Vedas – another religious tradition grew up, which probably had its roots in both the indigenous, pre-Aryan local culture and the Aryans' shamanistic past. This was the tradition of the ascetic, who was usually a member, not of the *brahmana*, but of the *kshatriya*, the warrior and aristocratic caste. Such warrior-ascetics – barred from an unmediated and unpatrolled relationship with the divine by the caste system – would renounce the world and, either singly or in groups, would hide themselves away in mountain or forest *asramas* (or *ashrams* – places of spiritual striving). Some were the forebears, no doubt, of modern *fakirs*, in search of supranormal powers. Most of them, however, were trying to find another and more personal way to the divine by abandoning the *Dharma* of the community. They mortified the flesh in various ways so that it could be subjugated by the mind. Meditation seems to have been practised and perhaps even yoga – images of figures sitting cross-legged in typically yogic fashion date from as far back as the period before the Aryan invasion.

The Four Stages of Life

What these ascetics were seeking was direct knowledge of the interpenetration of Brahman and *Atman* by means of self- (rather than drug-) induced states of exalted consciousness. It is reasonable to assume that many of those who were successful returned to their communities with a newly-acquired wisdom that flew in the face of the brahmin priesthood's proclaimed control over the gateway to religious experience. The response of the brahmins, though, was anything but aggressive. Instead, they began to incorporate elements of the ascetic philosophy into their own teachings and to lay down new rules that came to govern the ascetic path. They introduced the idea of the Four Stages of Life, by which a man was first a student, next a householder and then a patriarch who was finally able to start shaking off the bonds that tied him to the world. Only when he had done this – when he had fully paid his dues to *Dharma* – was he to be allowed to follow the *sanyassin's*, or renunciate's, way.

The texts in which the ascetics' philosophy and practices came to be enshrined were the Upanishads (or the Vedanta), composed between 800 and about 400 BC. Together with the Veda they encapsulate the two main Indo-Aryan paths to the divine: the priestly and the personal/ascetic. The Upanishads, though – particularly the later ones – represent a decline from the lofty and speculative mysticism of the early sages and poets. Brahman gradually became formalized and eventually took on the shape of the masculine Hindu creator-god Brahma; and *Atman*, instead of being both ineffable and universal, shrank in scale to become the permanent personal self or immortal soul (the *jivatman*) that transmigrates from one body to another after death according to the ancient law of *karma*.

The Sanskrit word *karma* has its roots in 'action', the willed action of body or speech or mind. The cosmic law of *karma* decreed – and still decrees in modern Hinduism – that the effects of past actions accumulate and disperse over several lifetimes. In the Upanishads, this law was conflated with the idea of the personalized *Atman*, so that from then on the status of a reborn individual was seen as being determined by the effects of his or her actions in past lives. (Thus an individual could be reborn as an animal, a human or even a spirit or minor god in a different dimension, depending on past deeds.) Today, different Hindu cults and sects have different notions of the ending of the soul's reiterative journey from one life to another. However, in the Upanishads it is the realization of the indivisibility of Brahman and *Atman* that finally releases an individual from the endless cycle of rebirth and suffering and nullifies once and for all the effects of past *karma*.

This, then, was the religious and social background against which prince Siddhartha Gautama, the future Buddha, was born. The nomadic Aryans had by this time (c.560 BC) spread out over India – although not without facing the sort of resistance recorded in such epics as the *Ramayana* and the *Mahabharata*, beloved of modern Hindus – and had settled down as agriculturalists. They had, in so far as the caste system allowed, integrated themselves with the local populations and had adopted many of their gods. There were thirty-three of these in the Brahmanist pantheon by the time of the Buddha's birth, all of them seen as separate manifestations of, and channels towards, the abstract Brahman. The creator-god Indra, for example, was believed to have sacrificed himself in order that the cosmos could be created out of his remains – thus necessitating the endlessly complicated sacrificial rituals of the brahmin priesthood, designed to guarantee its survival.

There was also considerable conflict, as we have seen, between the two religious traditions – priest-mediated and personal/ascetic – and it is tempting to believe that this may have been exacerbated by the great clearing of the Ganges plain which, by the time of Buddha's birth, had opened up vast and rich agricultural lands and had led to a new prosperity. The population had shot up, cities had emerged as important trading centres and there were new forms of political association, some of them tribal republics with leaders elected from the *kshatriya* caste – among them the Buddha's father. These may well have looked less kindly on brahminic orthodoxy than the iron-age kingdoms that were appearing elsewhere. But there were other pressures, too, that might have led many to favour the ascetic path in this new centre of Indian civilization – among them increased leisure, created by the accumulation of resources and personal insecurity brought on by a time of extreme change.

The Ascetic Groups

Whatever the pressures, though, it seems clear that more and more men were leaving home and becoming ascetics or *sramanas* (strivers) at around the time of the birth of Siddhartha Gautama. Identifiable heterodox sects, or groups of ascetics, were beginning to emerge by this time – each with its own philosophy and disciplines and each gathered around an individual teacher. Five main groups can be identified, according to John Snelling, the author of *The Buddhist Guidebook*:

1. Ajivakas: The teacher of the Ajivakas (or 'homeless ones') was Makkhali Gosala, who preached a totally determinist philosophy: The universe was a closed causal system but was little by little drawing each individual in it towards ultimate perfection – though the process would take aeons of time.

2. Lokayatas: The Lokayatas (or Materialists), gathered around Ajita Keshakambalin, believed that humans were composed of the four elements, into which they were re-resolved when they died. Death was the final ending for both the wise man and the fool, so in life men should seek all pleasures possible.

3. The Sceptics: The Sceptics held that brahminical doctrines were mutually contradictory and that ultimate truth was utterly unattainable. 'They are said to have wriggled like eels out of every question put to them', writes Snelling, 'but believed in cultivating friendliness and peace of mind'.

4. *The Jains*: The Jains, like the Lokoyatas, were contemporaries of Buddha in the sense that their philosophy seems to have been systematized by Mahavira in the second half of the sixth century BC – although its roots may go back a further thousand years. The Jains, in Snelling's words, 'held life to be an extremely painful business and aspired to attain *moksha* or liberation from the painful cycles of endless rebirth by withdrawing to a high, rarefied spiritual state'. They practised extreme forms of austerity and attached the highest value to the ethical life – a life of total honesty, chastity and non-attachment. They were also preoccupied with the karmic consequences of doing harm to any other living creature. They therefore rejected the sacrificial rituals that underpinned the Aryan/Brahmanic/Hindu view of the world; and many of them took the principle of *ahimsa* (or harmlessness) to extreme lengths to avoid violence towards even microscopic animals. Some would sweep the ground in front of them as they walked or wear masks over their mouths. They would go without clothes and filter their water. Some would even refuse to eat at all – and would starve themselves to a meritorious death. Although the Jains are still part of the religious life of India, few today, it is fair to say, are such radical ascetics.

5. The fifth sect – ultimately to spread over the whole continent of Asia – was that founded by Siddhartha Gautama, the Buddha, born, according to tradition, in the fourth month of the Indian calendar, a hundred miles north of the holy city of Benares, beneath the foothills

of the Himalayas – and it was in many ways the most radical and anti-clerical of them all. Although what later came to be called Buddhism had many features in common with the philosophy of the Jains, *Sakyamuni* – or the sage of the Sakha people, as the Buddha came to be called – went further. He forbade all intoxicants (such as *soma*); preached that there were no gods; and denied not only the existence of an eternal soul, essence or *Atman*, but also its ability to merge with the ultimate mystery of Brahman. He set his face against the blind following of teachers, including himself, preached in the ordinary language of the people and founded egalitarian communities that harked back in spirit to those that had existed before the Aryans had arrived. He was in his way, then, a social – as well as religious – revolutionary.

Chapter Two:

The Life Of Buddha:
The Path to Enlightenment

Such versions of the life of Buddha as we have were composed 500 years or more after his death. Even the earliest scriptures, those of the so-called Pali canon, which gathered together his teachings and precepts, contain nothing that can be called a biography. This is because the lore and traditions of Buddhism, during its first half-millennium, were passed on from one generation to another almost entirely by word of mouth. Stories were told and retold by wandering priests, monks or storytellers in a way that mixed theatre and religion. That is to say, village audiences learned Buddhism through the same sort of fabulous characters and divine beings that inhabit the *Ramayana* and the *Mahabharata*. The actual life of the Buddha himself was irrelevant to this process, *except in so far as it was enshrined in the telling of his teachings.*

Buddha's Life and Journey

By the time the first biography was actually written down – by a Sanskrit poet called Asvaghosa in the first or second century AD – the Buddha's life-story had accumulated an accretion of myth, legend and derring-do, which had turned its central character into a demigod, a supernatural figure out of epic. So, in the many later versions written after the *Buddhacarita* (or *Acts of the Buddha*), he was to remain. For all that, though, Buddha's very first biographer (as we know from the fragments of the *Buddhacarita*, in several Asian languages, that survive) regarded him as a real historical character. Beneath all the supranormal decoration of his own and later variations, there are the lineaments of a dramatic human story: of a man undergoing conflicts and temptations; trying out and rejecting different courses of action; exercising choice; and finally winning through – not by accident, or through any intervention of the gods, but by what he himself chooses to do. He is driven into action by compassion for suffering humanity. He is courageous, tough, supple-minded and, above all, extremely self-disciplined. He behaves throughout his long ordeals with the utmost sensitivity, delicacy and dignity.

Whatever else overlays this basic story – the trajectory of Buddha's life and journey – is also there for a purpose, we must assume, however far-fetched and fantastical it may seem to us today. The life is not only historical at root and highly moral in development but it is also a guidebook of the path towards enlightenment – in other words, it is a teaching manual.

Birth and Early Life

Great lives deserve great and important births – and so it was with Siddhartha Gautama, the prince and later sage (*Sakyamuni*) of the Sakya people, for he was conceived when his mother, Mahamaya (or Maya) dreamed that a Bodhisattva ('Buddha-to-be') came down from Tushita Heaven – the home, by tradition, of contented gods – and entered her body in the form of a white elephant with a red face.

During her pregnancy, which lasted for ten months, Mahamaya often meditated in Lumbini forest: it was there, in a grove of trees, that she finally gave birth from her side as she held on to the branch of a sacred tree. A great light covered the earth as the baby appeared, unstained and fully aware, and rain fell to wash both mother and child. Then the baby took seven steps, looked to the four corners of the world and said (in one of several versions): 'For enlightenment I was born, for the good of all that lives. This is the last time that I have been born into this world of becoming [*samsara*]. There is now no existence again.'

His mother died seven days later, her work in the world done, and from then on Siddhartha was raised by her sister Mahapajapati, who was perhaps another of his father's wives. It was soon clear that hers was no ordinary charge. At the baby's naming ceremony, his father arranged for his future to be predicted by a wise man called Asita, who found thirty-two auspicious marks on his body and prophesied that he would either become a powerful ruler – perhaps the monarch of the whole of India – or a great sage. If he took up the religious life and turned his back on his birthright, he said, Siddhartha could become a teacher of both men and gods, even the saviour of the world.

Father Suddhodana was not best pleased by this second possibility: he wanted Siddhartha to be a king. So, from then on, he did everything he could to make sure that he followed the warrior's rather than the ascetic's path. Arguing that his son's mind would only turn to religion if he saw and experienced the harsh and ugly realities of life, he created an environment of comfort, beauty and ease in which real life played no part. As Siddhartha got older, his father had three marble palaces built for him, one for each of the seasons, and in these he was confined to the upper floors, surrounded by every luxury and amenity wealth could buy – Benares silks, the finest oils, musicians, dancers and courtesans. Suddhodana wanted his son to be so ensnared in a life of privilege that he would never think to leave it.

For all this – all the pampering and spoiling – Siddartha grew up into a well-balanced, kind and studious young man, who was not only gifted in mathematics but also in sports and martial arts. It was by deploying these last talents of his that, at the age of sixteen, he won the hand in marriage of his beautiful young cousin Yasodhara. Yasodhara had been courted by a whole army of young princelings and aristocrats, but Siddhartha beat them all in a series of contests, in one of which he confidently drew a longbow that had belonged to an ancestor of his. The others couldn't even lift it.

In all this time, only one event disturbed the even tenor of Siddhartha's life. At the age of about seven, he went to a ploughing festival with his father, whose duty, as leader/king, was to plough the first furrow. As he watched from under the shade of a rose-apple tree, he saw how hard the men and animals worked and how the ploughs damaged plants and injured or killed small animals. He also saw a lizard eat an ant, only for it to be gobbled down by a snake, which was in turn soon snatched up by a vulture. As he pondered on these things, he experienced a sense of deep compassion and fell, almost without knowing it, into a pleasant meditative trance.

Perhaps it was the memory of this, preying on his mind throughout the years he spent in his palaces, within what was a happy marriage, that caused him to name his son, born when he was twenty-nine, Rahula (or 'fetter') – and to leave his life of luxury four times on four journeys of discovery.

The Four Sights

These expeditions into the outside world, made while his wife

Yasodhara was pregnant, were known to Buddhists everywhere as The Four Sights. On his first excursion, travelling with his charioteer Channa, he saw a frail old man. When he asked Channa what made the old man so weak and doddery, he was told that this was the eventual fate of all human beings, including himself. On the second journey, he saw a sick person: the response to his enquiry on this occasion was that illness could strike even the strongest and healthiest of individuals and there was nothing that could be done to prevent it. The third time he left the palace precincts he saw a corpse being stretchered to the cremation ground. When he asked what it was, he heard about death – an everyday event in human life, said Channa, since death itself was inevitable.

These three encounters had a deeply traumatic effect on Siddhartha, for he had become aware of the true facts of the human condition for the first time. Sickness, ageing and death were inescapable. Human life – all life – was dogged by impermanence, fear and pain. People had no control at all over their own fates and destinies. So how on earth could they pursue a life of pleasure or learning, thought Siddhartha, without coming to terms with this dreadful knowledge?

This was the starting-point for the longer journey that Siddhartha was ultimately to take, that of Seeing directly to the heart of the matter, just as it is for all Buddhists – clearing the mind of all its trivial preoccupations and pursuits and bringing into focus what is really important: that life is characterized by suffering. What happens after that point, in terms of the life one leads and the decisions one takes, is rooted in the knowledge that this is an absolutely fundamental problem that needs to be dealt with. Something must be done about it, but fatalism (passive acceptance) is not an option. The world that we routinely accept without thought is in reality a bizarre, cruel place and it is only by concentrating on this point, while determining to

25

transform our understanding of what it means to lead a human life within it, that we can fulfil our human potential.

The fourth journey that Siddhartha took with Channa provided him with the beginnings of a personal solution to this problem, for he saw for the first time a *sadhu* (a wandering holy man) who, although alone and dressed in rags, was apparently content with his lot. Even though he possessed nothing but a begging bowl, there was a tranquillity about him that other men, for all their possessions and family connections, lacked. Siddartha wanted to know the *sadhu*'s secret, but when he returned to the palace he realized that he could never do so without leaving his own pampered existence behind. If the *sadhu* was as unaffected by the fear of change and suffering (the realm of *samsara*) as he seemed to be, then it had to be because he had abandoned the material life to which he was attached. No spiritual solace was to be found in merely fulfilling one's social duties. The brahminic interpretation of *Dharma* was simply not enough.

The Great Renunciation

In other words, Siddhartha realized that if he was to find any sort of truth in life – if, like the *sadhu*, he was to learn to become indifferent to suffering – he would need to suffer himself. Not only would he have to give up his life of luxury but also the ties of duty and responsibility that linked him to his clan, his family, his father and his wife. He would have to make a commitment: it is with this act of commitment and renunciation that the life of each Buddhist begins. He would have to become a wanderer himself, a simple seeker after truth.

On the very night on which his son Rahula was born – according to the story – Siddhartha secretly left his palace with his charioteer for the last time. They rode to the river Anoma, the border of the Sakyas' territory with a neighbouring kingdom, and there Siddhartha took off his robes and jewels and handed them to Channa, telling him to return them to his father with news of his decision to search for salvation or die in the attempt. His father, he said, was not to grieve, since sooner or later they would have been separated by death anyway. Not knowing how much time he had left for his own life meant the search had to begin immediately. Channa tried to argue him out of it, but Siddartha would not be moved. Asvaghosa in his *Acts of the Buddha* gives Siddhartha a speech in which departure for the homeless life is justified as fidelity to an even higher *Dharma* than the one he had been brought up in.

With this, he cut off his hair and crossed the river, where he exchanged the clothes he still had for a passing hunter's. Siddhartha had now 'gone forth' in the same way that his followers were to do later. His search had started.

Siddhartha's Studies

For the next six years, according to the story, Siddhartha followed the ascetic path, begging for food and apprenticing himself to a succession of teachers who taught meditational techniques designed to achieve enlightenement (*bodhi*) and emancipation (*nirvana*). The first was Arada Kalama, who taught a form of meditation leading to 'the attainment of the state of nothing at all' and the second was Udraka Ramaputra whose aim was 'the attainment of neither perception nor non-perception'. It was clear, in other words, that as Siddhartha began his mendicant life he was not merely interested in the sort of contemplative identification of the individual soul and Brahman that was laid out in the Upanishads nor in the purgative and purifying abstinence of the Jains. What he sought was something more fundamental, the achievement of his goal of understanding through deep states of meditative concentration (*samadhi*). In later Hinduism this path became known as *raja-yoga* ('the royal discipline') – it was first outlined in the *Bhagavad Gita* in around 200 BC and was given its place of honour in the systematization of yogic practices in *the Yoga Sutras* five or six centuries later. But although Siddhartha became an adept at both forms – and was invited by his teachers to become a teacher himself – he ultimately abandoned them, unsatisfied, for *samadhi* alone could not provide him with the complete solution to his spiritual problem. It didn't reach far enough towards direct and perfect knowledge.

Next, he took himself off to the jungle, near a place called Uruvela, and began to submit his body to the cruellest of austerities and deprivations in an attempt to overcome the general suffering through his own and to exorcize all thoughts from his mind through self-denial. He spent long periods alone and naked – in 'the sky-blue state', as it was called. He endured every extreme of weather; he slept on beds of thorns; he experimented with an extreme form of meditation, holding his breath for as long as he could until he passed out and woke to blinding headaches; and he starved himself to the point of death. So extreme was his commitment that five other ascetics asked if they could join him in his strivings.

Little by little, though, Siddartha, who was by now all skin and bone, began to understand that he was getting nowhere. He was gaining in psychic powers but at the cost of his health – his survival, even – and he was getting no nearer to his goal of perfect understanding. He tried to think of another way, and he cast his mind back to the incident at the ploughing festival when, at the age of about seven, a feeling of compassion had spontaneously cast him into a pleasant meditative trance, a state of dispassionate equilibrium that was the first of the four stages of *dhyana*. Perhaps, he thought, this happy vision of childhood, free from all desire and sensuality, might provide an alternative way.

He also realized that if he went on mortifying his flesh in extreme ways, he might die and simply never find out, so when a woman came to the tree under which he sat and offered him food, he took it. When the five ascetics saw him eating – and continuing to eat – they soon left him in disgust, announcing that he had given up and abandoned the true path. But in fact Siddhartha had come to a profound decision.

The Middle Path

The memory of the childhood incident had begun to convince him that there was nothing wrong with being spiritually happy and he went on to understand, as he continued to eat each day, that a healthy body was also necessary to the pursuit of wisdom. Sensual self-indulgence might be a spiritual cul-de-sac – as he'd discovered for himself through The Four Sights – but so was mortification of the flesh. There was, however, a Middle Way – and this step towards enlightenment became central to the Buddhist *Dharma*. Happiness was important, after all, for the individual was not some sort of soul-substance carried by a greedy, machine-like body from which it had to be freed. Body and *Atman* formed an organic unity in which physical and psychic forces had their own parts to play.

The Temptation of Mara

According to the story of his life that is enshrined in the Buddhist tradition, Siddhartha then had five dreams that seemed to show that he was about to become a Buddha. At a place called Bodh Gaya in what is now the state of Bihar, he made himself a cushion of grass under a pipal tree, sat down facing east, and vowed never to rise again until he had reached enlightenment.

This vow – 'I will not rise from this spot until I am enlightened. Flesh may wither away, blood may dry up, but until I gain enlightenment I shall not move from this seat' – immediately attracted the attention of Mara and his hordes of demons. Mara, 'The Killer', is a sort of Buddhist Satan or Tempter, whose role is to maintain everything – desire, illusion and ignorance – that contributes to the realm of *samsara*, and he could not possibly tolerate the presence of a man who might not only find a way out of *samsara* but also a way to cheat Death himself. During the six years of striving, Mara had merely tried to whisper insinuations in Siddhartha's ear, but now he launched an all-out attack. As one colourful account has it:

> Mara ordered his army to attack Siddhartha with spears of copper, flaming swords and cauldrons of boiling oil. They came riding decaying corpses, and lashing out with hooks and whips and spiked wheels of fire. Some sprouted flames from every hair or rode mad elephants through the treetops. The earth shook and the regions of space flashed flames. Yet whenever anything touched him, it turned into a rain of flowers, fragrant and soft to the touch.

Siddhartha was protected by his merit, accumulated over several lifetimes, and by loving kindness, so the demons had to beat a retreat. At this point Mara himself went into action by using his magical powers. But he too was rebuffed and he was soon calling on his retinue to bear collective witness to the force of Siddhartha's merit. Siddhartha, having no witness of his own, touched the ground with his right hand – a familiar gesture in all Buddhist art – and called on the witness of

Mother Earth, who is said to have quaked in response to him.

Mara, having failed to force, scare or cow Siddhartha, had one last shot. He now sent in his three beautiful daughters – Discontent, Delight and Desire – to conjure up another army, this time of goddesses.

> Some of the goddesses veiled only half their face; some displayed their full round breasts; some teased him with half smiles; some stretched and yawned seductively; some deliberately appeared dishevelled; some sighed deeply with passion; some undressed slowly before him; some fingered their golden girdles; some swayed their hips like palm trees. And all whispered to him: 'Come and taste the delights of the world and forget nirvana and the path of liberation till you're old'.

Once more, though, the Buddha-to-be (*Bodhisattva*) remained impervious, and when dusk fell Mara's forces finally withdrew.

This story, a late addition to the Buddhist canon, contains a number of important psychological truths – for all its mythological form and shape. For there is no doubt that once a seeker decides to make his or her integrated, determined attempt on truth, the demons of fear are soon summoned. It is not only that old ingrained habits begin to shriek protest at their coming destruction, but there are other questions, such as 'What if I go mad or project myself into some bizarre psychic state'? There is terror in the face of the supernatural, death, and the entering of some sort of existential limbo. Good habits and preparation will, of course, see the seeker through, but then doubts about whether a seeker is up to the challenge begin to arise, doubts that can only be allayed by supreme self-confidence. The last peril of all, in the words of Richard H. Robinson and Willard L. Johnson, in their book *The Buddhist Religion: A Historical Introduction*, 'is of course the rosiest and the deadliest. Perfect love (*maitri*) may cast out fear, but it all too easily changes into personal pleasure'.

The Great Awakening

During the night, with a full moon over him and the temptations of Mara behind him, Siddhartha slowly climbed through the four stages of trance or *dhyana*, the first of which he had experienced as a child, gradually gaining greater concentration and control over his mind as he did so – a process sometimes described by Buddhists as 'letting go'. He was, we must imagine, using techniques taught him by his first two teachers, but he was reaching beyond them to the fourth stage, which was free from all opposites like pain and pleasure, knowledge and ignorance and where there was nothing but pure awareness, spiritual peace and direct unmediated insight meditation (*vipassana*), without any point of view.

There are few details in the narratives of Buddha about what he 'saw' or 'achieved' through this radical reshaping and redirection of perception, for it was obviously considered to be impossible to describe: in other words it was ineffable. All that is said is that Siddhartha remembered all his previous existences during the first watch of the night. In the second watch, he acquired the 'divine eye,' saw the whole universe as if in a mirror and penetrated right to the heart of its endless cycle of birth and dying. He acquired direct knowledge of *karma*, and saw how those who do good are given a happy rebirth while those who commit evil are doomed to a new round of misery.

In the third watch, says the narrative, he gained knowledge of the destruction of the *asavas* ('cankers', 'taints', 'binding influences'), generally understood as physical desire, desire for existence and ignorance. He perceived what came to be known as The Four Holy Truths: 'This is suffering, this is the source of suffering, this is the cessation of suffering, and this is the path that leads to the cessation of suffering'. His mind floated free of the *asavas* and, in the words of the Sutra, quoted by Robinson and Johnson, he saw that 'In me emancipated arose knowledge of my emancipation. I realised that rebirth has been destroyed, the holy life has been lived, the job has been done, there is nothing after this'. As the morning star rose after his long night, he looked out at the world with new eyes, like a man waking up from a dream. He had become the Buddha (the 'emancipated' or 'awakened' one), and he again touched the ground for the earth to bear witness.

Chapter Three:

The Legacy of Enlightenment

Various supernatural events are supposed to have occurred at the moment of the Buddha's Enlightenment. The earth, it was said, swayed like a drunken woman. There were claps of thunder; rain fell; breezes blew; and blossoms and fruit dropped from the sky as Buddha's ancestors applauded his victory and offered him reverence from paradise.

Afterwards, according to the legend, the Buddha remained under the pipal – now the *Bodhi* or Enlightenment – tree for another week, and then spent a further forty-two days in the vicinity, meditating and doing yogic exercises. He was debating within himself whether, and how, to pass on what he had learned, what he had now become. At first he was reluctant, for he knew, on the basis of his own two apprenticeships, that truth cannot be taught, only experienced directly. He also believed that people would find it hard to understand his *Dharma* or live by it, so attached were they to their illusions and wordly ties. Inviting them to accept a truth that undermined and threatened their whole way of life would be nothing but a waste of energy.

In the end, though, his compassion for their unnecessary

suffering tipped the balance – as did a visit from Brahma, the highest god in the popular pantheon of the time. Brahma left the Brahma-world, and appeared before him to announce:

> May the Blessed One teach the Dharma. May the Well-gone One teach the Dharma. There are living beings with a little dust in their eyes who fall away through not hearing the Dharma. They will be recognizers of the Dharma.

At this point, it is said, Buddha opened up his Buddha-eye to survey the world and saw that it was indeed true – many people were impure and dull, but there were some people with keen minds and considerable purity of heart who might well accept his message. Where, though, to begin? He thought of his two teachers, but saw that they had recently died. Then he thought of the five ascetics who had earlier shared his extreme austerities. When he located them in the Deer Park at Isipatana (modern Sarnath) near Benares – over a hundred miles from where he was – he decided to join them.

On his journey to Isipatana, the story continues – as told in the *Sutras*, the collected writings of the Buddhist canon – he met a wandering ascetic who remarked on his clear eyes and shining complexion, and asked what discipline he followed. The Buddha replied that he was a Victor (*Jina*) and that he had no equal in the world of gods and men – he was omniscient and had reached *nirvana*. The mendicant answered with a single syllable – which meant 'It may be so', or 'Let it be so' – and promptly walked away to take another road. In other words, the Buddha was rejected by the first man to whom he offered himself.

When he finally reached the Deer Park at Isipatana (Sarnath) and met up with his one-time fellow-strivers, they too were at first dismissive. He was, after all, the backslider who had given up the ascetic path to indulge his body. But they were soon overwhelmed by his newly-acquired charisma, and in the end they welcomed him, took his bowl and staff, prepared a seat for him among them and gave him water to wash his feet. They called him 'Friend Gautama', but the Buddha immediately stopped them and said that he was now a *Tathagata* ('Teacher', 'one who has reached what is really so'), a perfectly enlightened *arhant* (usually translated as 'saint'). He had reached the ultimate, immortal truth, the *Dharma*, he said, and he was going to preach it. If they followed what he taught, they could then realize it for themselves. Finally, after much initial scepticism, the five men agreed to listen to him.

The Four Noble Truths and the Eightfold Path

We cannot know whether what is called by tradition the Discourse (*darsana*) of the Four Noble Truths actually took place on this occasion – we know as little about it as we do of Jesus's Sermon on the Mount – although it does seem appropriate enough for Buddha's audience of five ascetics. Part of his message was the message of The Middle Way: sensual indulgence was world-tied, illusory and spiritually useless, but mortification and self-torture were no better. It was the Middle Way, requiring vigilance but avoiding extremes, that led to enlightenment and *nirvana*. This Middle Way, he said, was the way of the Holy Eightfold Path, which he described as:

1. right understanding
2. right intention
3. right speech
4. right conduct

5. right livelihood
6. right effort
7. right mindfulness
8. right concentration

He then declared the Four Noble Truths to his audience. The first was the truth of *dhukka*, a Pali word that means 'suffering' but also contains within it overtones of impermanence, imperfection and unsatisfactoriness. This kind of suffering, he said, was to be found at every level and in every aspect of existence. Birth, illness, decay, death, living with one's enemies, being separated from one's loves – the whole world as it is experienced through the five *skandhas* (forms of perception) – was marked and dogged by this suffering.

The second Noble Truth was the truth of the cause of suffering – the intolerable neural itch of desire or craving, for pleasure, for life, sometimes even for death – and the third Truth was the truth of its cessation. When such desires or cravings were completely extinguished – by renunciation, dispassion and non-dependence – then the suffering, too, would come to an end. The fourth Noble Truth was the truth of the path leading towards this cessation of suffering – and with this the Buddha, in what may well have been his first sermon, seemed to come full circle. For this was the truth of the Eightfold Path, which would bring freedom from desires, end suffering in this life and interrupt the endless cycle of an individual's birth and rebirth into the world.

In this way, Buddha revealed for the first time the purified true knowledge he had seen at the moment of his Enlightenment. He did not claim to have created it – it had always existed. But by apprehending it and now teaching it – as others, now forgotten, had done in the past – he was beginning to turn the wheel of *Dharma* once more. One of his audience, a man called Kaundinya, grasped the totality of this as the Buddha was still speaking: he was said to have suddenly acquired the pure *Dharma*-eye. 'Kaundinya has got it! Kaundinya has got it!' exclaimed the Buddha, and when Kaundinya asked to be ordained as a disciple, the Buddha confirmed him with the simple words: 'Come, *bhikkhu* ['monk'], the Dharma is well proclaimed. Walk the holy pathway to the perfect termination of suffering.' *Sangha*, the Buddhist community, had been born.

The Building of the *Sangha*

The Buddha later gave another sermon to his small, select audience, this time on the five so-called *skandhas* – form, feeling, conception, dispositions and consciousness – the interpenetrative ways in which we perceive the material world and the world presents itself to us (a theme to which I shall return later). All of these, he said, were *anatman* ('devoid of self'): they were part of the realm – and causation – of suffering. On hearing this, the other four men in the Deer Park not only became members of the Buddha's order of *bhikkus*, but – according to the tradition – free from the world of illusions: *arhants*, or saints.

Soon, others came to the Deer Park to hear him, among them a young man called Asa, the world-weary son of a rich Benares merchant, to whom Buddha taught a version of the *Dharma* suitable for laymen, before introducing him finally to the Four Truths and allowing him to be ordained. Asa's father soon followed his son, and it was he who became the first Buddhist lay follower (or *upasaka*) by making a formal commitment to the Three Refuges as a rite of entry, reciting three times:

I go for refuge to the Buddha
I go for refuge to the Dharma
I go for refuge to the Sangha

He was followed in turn by his wife and daughters, who became the first female lay followers (*upasika*), and by fifty of Asa's young male friends, who listened to the Buddha and were subsequently ordained, having freed themselves from the shackles of perception to become *arhants* – as had Asa.

Asa and his friends, the five ascetics and Buddha himself formed the core of what became a missionary movement in northern and central India. They left Sarnath and travelled from village to village and city to city, proclaiming the Buddha's teachings 'for the the benefit of the many, out of compassion for the world, for the welfare of gods and humans'. Men and women 'with keen faculties will attain liberation', said the Buddha, 'if – and only if – they actually hear the *Dharma* message'.

Right from the beginning, the great strength of Buddhism was its openness to all, regardless of race, caste, class or gender. The Brahmanic schools kept their teachings as esoteric and secret as possible and the masters maintained close control over their students. They also used an archaic form of Sanskrit. By contrast, the early Buddhists spoke in ordinary demotic dialect and broadcast their message to anyone and everyone to whom it could be communicated. The result was electrifying. People began travelling long distances for ordination: so many of them, in fact, and at such hardship to themselves, that Buddha soon gave his monks permission to confer ordination themselves wherever they went. The result was that the *Sangha* became self-replicating: word spread like wildfire over wide distances, far wider than could be controlled by any single authority.

And it wasn't only individuals who were prepared to give up their lives to the Buddhic *Dharma* – there were also whole sects. For example, one early convert was the leader of a fire-worshipping sect of ascetics, Uruvela Kasyapa, whom the Buddha so impressed with his supranormal powers that he and his five hundred followers immediately entered the Buddhist fold – to be followed soon afterwards by his two ascetic brothers and five hundred devotees of their own. Two members of another sect, who were later to become Buddha's chief disciples – Sariputta, famous for his wisdom, and Moggallanna, celebrated for his psychic powers – brought with them into the *Sangha* two hundred of their fellow-strivers who had become unsatisfied, as they themselves had, with the teachings of the master they had followed.

At first the Buddha made no strict rules for new converts like these. He simply asked ordinands to commit themselves to the Three Refuges and to an ethical life. They had to promise:

- not to harm any living thing
- not to take anything that wasn't freely given
- to forsake the world of fleshly pleasures and stay celibate
- to speak and think truthfully, kindly and compassionately
- to shun all intoxicants.

Later Buddha instituted a more formal ordination ceremony, which consisted of shaving off head and facial hair, ritually taking up the yellow robe and promising to obey certain simple monastic rules (subsequently expanded and written up in great detail in the *Vinaya Pitaka*). But in the early days the code of the monks seems to have remained simple, their purpose clear. For nine months of the year they were to travel as mendicants, pursuing their own paths and spreading the word as missionaries. But for three months, during the Monsoon or rainy season, they were free to go into retreat – which they did, often in each other's company. This was the seed-bed out of which grew the Buddhist monastery.

The First Monasteries

Buddha spent the first rainy season at Sarnath and soon afterwards travelled to Rajagaha, the capital of Magadha, where he was welcomed by King Bimbisara and a great crowd of people, all of whom – says tradition – became lay followers. The next day the king himself waited on the Buddha and his *bhikkhus* at the alms meal, and afterwards he gave a pleasure garden to the *Sangha* outside the city called The Bamboo Grove, where a rich merchant later put up shelters. Here, in the first makeshift monastery, the Buddha spent the next two Rains Retreats, as they came to be called. But for the fourth he was invited to Savatthi, the capital of the neighbouring kingdom of Kosala. His host there was a rich philanthropist called Anathapindika, who bought for the purpose another pleasure-garden owned by a nobleman called Jeta – and hence called Jetavana or 'Jeta's Grove'. A second monastery was subsequently built here and was soon followed by a third, the Pubbarama or 'Eastern Park', built on land, also near Savatthi, donated by a rich laywoman named Visakha. When the Buddha settled permanently at Savatthi, he spent alternate Rains Retreats at the Jetavana and the Pubbarama.

After the fourth Rains Retreat, the Buddha made a journey back into his past: he went to visit his family and people in the Sakya capital of Kapilavatthu. For his father Suddhodana the visit of the *Sakyamuni* (the 'sage of the Sakya people') was a bitter-sweet occasion, for though he himself was set on the Path by his son, he lost another of his children, Nanda (the son of Buddha's aunt and foster-mother, Mahapajapati), as well as his beloved grandson, Buddha's son Rahula, to conversion and ordination. (Rahula went on to become a leading light among the trainers of new monks and novices.) He complained bitterly to the Buddha about this and won from him a small concession: he agreed that children would no longer be ordained without their parents' agreement.

These, though, were not the only relatives who chose to follow the Buddha, for around this time his cousin Ananda – who was to remain his faithful attendant for the rest of his life – became an ordained monk. Also, after Suddhodana died the following year, his widow Mahapajapati, who had raised the Buddha, begged to be accepted as a nun. She asked three times and was three times refused. But so determined was she that she cut off all her hair, put on the yellow robe and followed him along the road to a neighbouring kingdom with a retinue of ladies-in-waiting. There, Ananda took pity on the women's wretched, travel-worn state and intervened with the Buddha, who finally, and reluctantly, consented. He told Ananda that women had exactly the same spiritual potential as men, but he imposed eight stringent rules on Mahapajapati and the nuns (*bhikkhunis*) who were to follow her into the *Sangha* – among them her attendants and the wife of King Bimbisara – one of which was the acknowledgment that even the most senior nun was still junior to a monk, even one who had been ordained that very day.

His concern, he later told Ananda, was that the presence of women would distract the monks – and indeed he later warned his *bhikkus* to be vigilant in their presence. When Ananda asked how monks should behave when nuns were about, Buddha is recorded as having said they should not talk and they should keep their eyes open. It may have been around this time that he began to increase the number of promises each ordinand, male and female, had to make before admission to the *Sangha*, and to lay down the complex rules – governing every aspect of their behaviour – that are recorded in the Vinaya Pitaka. These rules were considered to be so all-important that, in the early history of the Buddhist community, they even took precedence over the Buddha's teachings. Morality – right conduct – came before everything else.

Buddha's Mission

For almost half a century the Buddha worked as a missionary, wandering from village to village for nine months of each year. When he arrived at a settlement, he would wait quietly with his alms bowl at its inhabitants' doors until he had gathered enough food for his one meal of the day. Then he would go off to a mango grove on the outskirts to eat, and would be joined there afterwards by anyone and everyone who wanted to hear him preach. Virtually his whole life, in other words, consisted of encounters with ordinary people of every caste and class, either met on the road or at village meetings. Many of these encounters passed into the Buddhist canon, each with its own moral or spiritual lesson. One of these, for example – as retold in Ven. Sangharaskshita's *A Guide to the Buddhist Path* – was with a brahmin:

> Journeying along the high road, the Buddha met a man called Dona [who was] skilled in the science of bodily signs. Seeing on the Buddha's footprints the mark of a thousand-spoked wheel, he followed in his track along the road until he eventually caught up with the Buddha, who was sitting beneath a tree. As the Buddha was fresh from

his Enlightenment, there was a radiance about his whole being. We are told that it was as though a light shone from his face – he was happy, serene, joyful. Dona was very impressed by his appearance, and he seems to have felt that this wasn't an ordinary human being, perhaps not a human being at all. Drawing nearer, he came straight to the point, as the custom is in India where religious matters are concerned. He said, 'Who are you?'

Now the ancient Indians believed that the universe is stratified into various levels of existence, that there are not just human beings and animals, as we believe, but gods, and ghosts, and yaksas, and gandharvas, and all sorts of other mythological beings, inhabiting a multi-storey universe, the human plane being just one storey out of many. So Dona askled, 'Are you a yaksa?' (a yaksa being a rather terrifying sublime spirit living in the forest). But the Buddha said, 'No'. Just 'No'. So Dona tries again. 'Are you a gandharva?' (a sort of celestial musician, a beautiful singing angel-like figure). Once again the Buddha said 'No', and again Dona asked, 'Well then, are you a deva?' (a god, a divine being, a sort of archangel). 'No'. Upon this Dona thought, 'That's strange, he must be a human being after all'. And he asked him that too, but yet again the Buddha said 'No'. By this time Dona was thoroughly perplexed, so he demanded, 'If you are not any of these things, then who are you?' The Buddha replied, 'Those mental conditionings on account of which I might have been described as a yaksa or a gandharva, as a deva or a human being, all those conditionings have been destroyed by me. Therefore I am a Buddha'.

Another much-celebrated encounter was with a woman called Kisagotami whose only son had died and who was wandering about, distraught, with his body in her arms – here told in an embellished version quoted by Clive Erricker in his *Teach Yourself Buddhism*.

> Kisagotami was almost driven out of her mind by her sorrow. A wise man saw her . . . and realised how much she needed help. He had heard some of the teaching of Gotama Buddha, and thought that he might be able to help her come to terms with her grief. He approached Kisagotami gently and told her that the Buddha was staying nearby and that he might have medicine for her son. 'Go and ask him', he said. Kisagotami went to find the Buddha and stood on the edge of the crowd, listening to him. When she had the chance, she called out to him, 'O, Exalted One, give me medicine for my son'.
>
> Part of the Buddha's greatness lay in his skill in knowing how to help other people. He told her kindly to go to the city nearby and visit every house. 'Bring me some grains of mustard seed from every household in which no-one has ever died.'
>
> Kisagotami was delighted. Here was someone who took her seriously. She went to the city, knocked [at] the first house and asked for some grains of mustard seed from the householder, if no-one had ever died there. The householder told her with great sadness that he had recently lost his wife. Kisagotami listened to his story with growing sympathy, understanding his grief from her own. She eventually moved on, but found that in every house there was a story of sickness, old age and death. Her own

grief seemed different now that she shared that of others, and she realised that the Buddha had known when he sent her out that she would find that her predicament was the common experience of human beings. Death is the law common to all that lives. She now took the body of her dear little son to the cremation ground and let it be cremated, fully realising that all is impermanent.

Kisagotami then returned to the Gotama Buddha. He asked her whether she had brought him the grains of mustard seed. She told him what had happened, and what she had realised. She then asked him to accept her as his follower and to teach her more about the nature of reality and the path to understanding . . .

Early Buddhic literature teems with encounters of this kind. There was Katyayana, a Brahmin court-priest sent by the king of Avanti in western India to find out more about the Buddha – he was sent back as monk and *arhant* to spread word of the *Dharma* in the West (and to become the first Buddhist commentator, 'foremost of those who analyze at length what the Buddha has stated concisely'). There were kings and queens, Jains and Brahmanists – and even a well-known and murderous bandit called Angulimala, or 'Finger-Necklace', so called because he wore his victims' fingers in a gruesome trophy round his neck. One day he gave chase to the Buddha as he was travelling on a deserted stretch of road, but however fast he ran he still could not catch him. So he shouted out, 'Hey! Stop, monk!', at which the Buddha coolly replied, 'But I have stopped, Angulimala. Isn't it time you stopped [using violence] too?' Angulimala promptly threw away his sword and, like so many others in the Canon, begged to be allowed to become one of Buddha's followers.

The Death of the Buddha

By the time he was seventy-nine, the Buddha knew that his body was failing, but he still would not let up. That season he travelled from Rajagaha by a series of stages to Vaisali in the northwest, preaching along the way. He stopped at Nalanda, where a great Buddhist university was later built, and at Pataligama, where he prophesied the creation of a great new city – now modern Patna.

Once at Vaisali, though, he became seriously ill with 'violent and deadly pains', and it was only by an act of supreme will that he was able to suppress them. He had not yet made any formal farewell to the *Sangha* – on whose survival his thoughts seemed to be running at that time, for he told his faithful cousin and attendant Ananda that he did not want the community to be personally dependent on him in any way. Each *bhikkhu* had to be as self-reliant as possible, he said, and should turn to the *Dharma* if in any doubt. He had taught them everything they needed to know. There were no extra dimensions, no esoteric teachings that had been somehow withheld. They already knew everything that was necessary.

When the rains let up, he moved on to one of the first monasteries, Jeta's Grove in Savatthi, where he heard the news of the death of Sariputta, one of his most cherished disciples. (Another, the adept psychic Moggallanna, seems to have died at about the same time.) This may have dispirited him, for back in Vaisali, according to *The Sutra of the Great Decease*, he hinted to Ananda that he had the power to prolong his life more or less indefinitely, if (and only if) he was asked. Ananda failed to seize the moment – for which he was later much blamed by the *Sangha* – and from then on the Buddha seems to have lost the will to live, for the death process began in earnest. When Mara ('The Killer') came near and told him it was time for him to attain *paranirvana* (perfect, or final *nirvana*), the Buddha simply agreed. He said, 'Don't fuss, Evil One. Very soon – within three months – the Tathagata's *paranirvana* will take place.'

Once more he set off, however, travelling from village to village, preaching at a place called Pava before receiving the meal that finally killed him, from a man called Cunda the Smith. It was of minced pork or mushrooms – scholars disagree – and it caused 'violent sickness, bleeding and acute stomach pain'. Somehow he managed to travel onwards towards Kusinagara, an insignificant village in the country of the Mallas (now Kasia in Uttar Pradesh), but outside it, in a grove of sala trees, he collapsed. He asked Ananda to make him a bed between two of the trees and he lay on it on his right side, with his head, supported by his hand, to the north and his face to the west, in a posture widely celebrated in Buddhist iconography.

He went on teaching through the night, according to the legend, even giving instruction to a wandering ascetic called Subhadra, who became the last of his converts to be accepted into the *Sangha*. Ananda was upset by this interruption of his last hours and wept. But the Buddha said to him, 'Don't mourn. Haven't I told you it's in the nature of things that we're separated from those we hold most dear? So why be upset?' He promised Ananda, who was not yet an *arhant*, that he would be 'liberated' soon. As to the question of his successor, he said to Ananda in the words of the *Digha-Nikaya*:

> As I have never sought to direct or subject the community
> to my teachings, I leave no such instruction to the Sangha.
> I am reaching my end. After my death each of you will be
> your own island, your own refuge. Take no other refuge.

The *Dharma* itself, in other words, was to be the Buddha's true successor.

By this time the Buddha was surrounded by monks, by local tribespeople and, according to legend, the lamentations of nature and of the gods, who were gathered around him so densely 'that a hair could not be slipped between them'. When his teaching was done, he asked three times if his disciples had any last questions or doubts. They were all silent. Then he spoke his last words to them: 'All created things are impermanent by nature. Work diligently towards your own salvation.' He then went into trance and climbed through the stages of *dhyana* until he reached the fourth, from which he passed into *paranirvana*. He died at the age of 80, free from rebirth, on the night of the July full moon, in the meditative calm in which he had learned to live.

The Funeral of the Buddha

The next day the people of Kusinagara and the surrounding area arrived to bury him according to the old Aryan tradition. The wake went on for six days with music, dancing and the offering of garlands and scents. The body was washed and anointed with oil and then wrapped in alternate layers of cotton wool and cloth. Eight chiefs of the Mallas then carried it on a bier to a tribal shrine, and there it was cremated – though not without some difficulty for the pyre, traditionally lit by the eldest son, would not catch fire until his senior living disciple, the ascetic Mahakasypa, arrived to light the first torch.

Before he lit it, though, Mahakasypa wanted to say goodbye and to pay homage to his beloved teacher by kissing his feet – still a practice in modern India. Immediately the bindings on the Buddha's feet unravelled, it was said, and after Mahakasypa had made his obeisance, the pyre caught light spontaneously and burned itself out without any human intervention. The Buddha's bones, though, turned out to be indestructible, according to the Canon, and some of them at least were buried in a *stupa* (memorial mound) raised at a nearby crossroads.

It was a funeral fit for an Aryan king. In fact, the rites echoed those of Homeric Greece – Hector's funeral in *The Iliad*, for example – and the *stupa* was exactly the same sort of 'round' barrow that was used to house the bodies of bronze-age kings and chieftains in places that were as far apart as Orkney and the East. It was also royal in another sense, too, for no distinction was made between the sacred and the secular realms at all – neither in Sanskrit nor in Pali nor in Ardamagadhi, the colloquial language the Buddha probably spoke. The same word, *arya* (Aryan), was used for both 'noble' and 'saint', and *puja* was used for both 'honour, respectful reverence' and for 'worship'. Buddha, then, was the true equivalent or equal of 'a king' or 'a noble' since the two spheres were undifferentiated – as were, in the popular view, the holy men whose *stupas* and shrines (*caitya*), where honour/reverence/worship was offered, dotted the countryside.

Because of this, there seems to have been considerable squabbling about the final disposition of the Buddha's relics, before the funeral party went its way. The Mallas laid claim to them, since the Buddha had died on their territory and they had arranged and conducted the funeral. But powerful leaders from other areas also wanted to lay their hands on them, since not only were they sacred, but they would also convey prestige and the mantle of authenticity – closeness to Buddha – on their caretakers. (They were also, one has to say, a potential source of revenue from worshippers and pilgrims.) The matter was decided, on the brink of a very un-Buddha-like battle, by an agreement to divide the relics, which were later granted their own individual monument or temple. The great building programme of the Buddhist community – and the myriad representations of the Buddha in sculptural form – had begun.

The Life as Example

The life of the Buddha is the cornerstone of Buddhism, just as the life (and death) of Jesus is that of Christianity, for his is literally the model life, the life on which the life of Buddhists is modelled. In this sense, his life and teachings are one, as he himself recognized when he said: 'Whoever sees *Dharma* sees me; whoever sees me sees *Dharma*.'

The trajectory of his life – presented as that of an epic hero in the battle for spiritual knowledge and self-realization – is a demonstration of the way actions and values are co-dependent. In its first part, the young Siddhartha, as his father's heir, is set to inherit the physical world. He is indulged, given everything that could possibly satisfy him. His palaces and lifestyle represent the fleeting world of materiality (*samsara*), the realm of impermanence, suffering, death and inevitable rebirth in an extreme, and perhaps enviable, form.

The first three of the Four Sights – his very first contacts with old age, sickness and death – enable him to realize that everything he has held to be of value up until this time is, in fact, meaningless. The fourth of the Sights – his encounter with the ascetic 'striver' – points to the way out. By completely changing his life, he is now able to begin to take personal responsibility for his values and actions. He learns self-discipline and steeps himself in the techniques of self-transformation that were available at the time. Like a spiritual physician, he has now not only identified the disease and realized that it can be cured, but he is also beginning to find where the cure lies.

The six years he spends as an ascetic and *yogi* are a time of intense self-reflection, of learning, and lead to the choices implicit in the Middle Way. He resolves for himself what values will govern his life, and through the visions of the Enlightenment he is ultimately transformed. The disease that he has identified at the root of human life has now been finally – and permanently – beaten.

After the Enlightenment, he decides to return to the world, to share these new values of his – his cure – and to exemplify for his fellow countrymen the spiritually considered and humane actions that spring from them. After almost fifty years of work as a missionary, he faces death with equanimity and dies with immense calm, without any of the anxieties of those still tied to the world.

His life, therefore, exemplifies the three-fold nature of what is known as the Buddhist Path. Everyone is born into a particular family or culture and makes accommodations and adjustments to them, gradually accumulating habits and tastes in the process which foreordain that we will behave in a particular way. Our lives, in other words, become progressively circumscribed and depotentialised. All we can do about it is to start again – either passively, by means of rebirth, or actively, by confronting this fact and taking counter-action. If we refuse to take this second option – refuse to become aware of the problem as the Buddha did – then there can be no spiritual maturity in this or any other life. We can never be free as individuals.

The ideal Buddhist way of dealing with this is patterned directly on the Buddha's own experience. It starts with a curative morality (*sila*), a set of ethical rules designed to purge and purify the individual and bring him or her closer to his or her essential nature. The following of this moral path is the beginning of transformation, since it increases self-knowledge and awareness (or mindfulness, *smrti*), without which we can never come to terms with the underlying illness – the causes and effects of our own past actions and assumptions. Essential too is mental discipline (*samahdi*), the cultivation of meditative calm (*samatha*) and what is called one-point concentration.

Samahdi leads, in a sense, to the third element, *prajna*, or wisdom, which consists in directly perceiving the truth of the *Dharma* and of Buddhist life-values. But wisdom – and its getting – is not really seen as separable, a different kind of milestone, from either *sila* or *samahdi*, for each is unattainable without the other two. The moral life, for example, cannot be sustained without both mental discipline and wisdom, and wisdom itself is also acquired cumulatively rather than in an all-at-once sort of way. It is a quality that grows as thought and understanding become gradually freed from ignorance, and this unchaining of the individual can only be achieved by following the three-fold path as a whole. The end result, the ultimate goal, was described by Buddha to his faithful Ananda not long before he died (in a version quoted in Clive Erricker's *Teach Yourself Buddhism*):

> Those who have died after the complete destruction of the three bonds, of lust, of covenance, and of the egotistical cleaving to existence, need not fear the state after death. They will not be in a state of suffering; their minds will not continue as a Karma of evil deeds or sin, but are assured of final deliverance. When they die nothing will remain of them but their good thoughts, their righteous acts, and the bliss that proceeds from truth and righteousness. As rivers must at last reach the distant main, so their minds will be reborn in higher states of

existence and continue to press on to their ultimate goal, which is the ocean of truth, the eternal peace of Nirvana.

The ideal Buddhist course, then, for lay person and monk alike, follows a progression closely modelled on the life and mental development (*bhavana*) of Buddha – except that for the lay person, of course, the final destination will take longer.

Chapter Four:

Buddhism as Taught by Buddha

Thus have I heard. The Blessed One was once living in the Deer Park at Isipatana [the Resort of Seers] near Varanasi [Benares]. There he addressed the group of five *bhikkhus*.

So begins the first discourse of the Buddha, as it appears in the collected writings of the Buddhist canon, the Sutras. The word *sutra* means thread – each Sutra is thus a thread in the whole tapestry of Buddhic thought, and this discourse is perhaps the most important thread of all, since it lays out the Four Noble Truths and the Middle Way, the kernel of everything the Buddha had learned in the years up to and including his Enlightenment. In that time he had gained intimate experience of both sensual pleasure and self-mortification and he described both here as 'unworthy and unprofitable'. (Self indulgence was also 'low, common and the way of ordinary people', and self-mortification was 'painful'.) The correct path to follow, he said, was the Middle Way between them, which alone led to 'vision, knowledge, calm, insight, enlightenment and *nirvana*'.

The Middle Way was also the fourth of the Four Noble Truths and it is worth looking at them in turn in order to see Buddhism clearly for what it is: a doctrine of salvation.

Part One: Buddhism in the Time of Buddha

The First Noble Truth: All Is Suffering

'Suffering' is a very approximate, and somewhat misleading, translation of the complex word *dukkha*, for Buddha acknowledged that life was not just one long vale of tears: it also had its moments of happiness. What he was saying was that when a human life is looked at overall, it is clear that what we might call a permanent state of *angst*, which stems from what we want and hope for ourselves, is *systematically* built into it. This desire for ourselves causes *angst* (or *dukkha*, suffering), because even if we get what we want we are aware that we cannot have it for ever: so we not only suffer in the anticipation of our desires but also in their loss. If we do not get what we want we still suffer, but this time from dissatisfaction and thwarted longing. A fundamental, built-in anxiety is part of the human experience, in other words. If we set goals for ourselves and fail to reach them, we become miserable; and if we do reach them, we want more – enough is never enough. And over all this web of desire and frustration hangs the presence of sickness, old age and death which casts a pall of anxiety over ourselves and all our relationships. Life, to sum up – and to appropriate Oscar Wilde's epigram about the smoking of cigarettes – may sometimes be exquisite, but it still leaves you (spiritually) unsatisfied, unfulfilled.

The answer to this problem, said the Buddha, cannot lie in changing the world to accommodate our desires and dreams. It must instead lie in ourselves, for the condition of the world is part of the problem, not part of the solution. The world is, by its very nature, impermanent (*anicca*) and subject to change. A state of endless fluctuation is systematically built into it which prevents everything and anything from enduring, so that nothing at all – no moment, no feeling, no thought, no action, no person – can last. However hard we try to create permanence for ourselves, therefore, it must always slip through our fingers. The Buddha said that death is, of course, the major under-cutter of this permanence, but little deaths and new beginnings fill every minute of existence – it is simply the nature of the world we live in, in which change is both necessary and inevitable. In the realm of *samsara*, therefore – the world of daily life – there *can* only be impermanence and *dukkha*. This description, from the Buddhic point of view, is neither happy nor sad, neither optimistic nor pessimistic. It is simply *so*.

The Second Noble Truth: The Origin of Suffering (or *Angst*)

The Second Noble Truth goes deeper into the roots of *dukkha*, into the way in which we confront the world through an organized personality we call 'the self' or 'I'. It is, in a sense, a psychological theory of relativity.

Put into its simplest form, the essential cause of *dukkha*, said Buddha, was *tanha* (or thirst). This thirst can be described as a fundamental, in-wired longing for something outside ourselves, and it ranges from gross manifestations like greed, lust and miserliness to more subtle and seemingly benign ones – like wanting to do good in the world or to know the truth. One way and another, Buddha said, we are victims of what the poet W. H. Auden called, in another context, an 'intolerable neural itch,' a constant desire to move our 'selves' out into the world in order to direct, change or understand 'it'.

But what exactly are these 'selves'? And what is the 'it' out there that we want to intervene in? In ordinary parlance we routinely separate the two concepts. We talk of 'the world I live in' and take it for granted that this 'I' of ours is somehow detached from its environment, and that the self or ego is a privileged, inside observer of people and events; the whole passing show. But how true can this be in reality, when everybody else 'out there' is carrying around their own selves, their own egos, and believing exactly the same thing? We ordinarily compensate for this unsettling fact by making remarks like 'Well, everyone has their own point of view' and other bromides, but we fail to fully examine its implications. Instead, we continue to believe – in a muddled, anxious and *systematic* state of *dukkha* – that we are somehow the centre of the universe.

But are we? And *can* we be? This, essentially, was Buddha's question – and it is a question that recurs in our daily lives, insinuating itself willy-nilly into our consciousnesses. Relativity, that is to say, keeps creeping in. Imagine the 'I', for example, as a person standing alone on a station platform when a train comes through. Believing that he is fixed in some way, permanent, assured of his 'I'-ness, he observes the train, the engine, the carriages, the people travelling between departure and destination, their lives changing in the process. Yet to a person on the train looking out of the window, his 'I' is just a momentary presence, then a past image, a distant memory. For each 'I', in other words, it is the other which is fleeting, transient – their realities are contradictory.

What Buddha said in effect was that neither of these two people, these two 'Is', is at all permanent in the way in which we imagine as individuals that they must be. What is moving is neither the train nor the person left behind on the platform, but that other great vehicle that sweeps through both platform and train – all life – alike: time.

Let us create another analogy by imagining the 'I' as a person standing on earth looking up at the sky, examining a star. He knows enough about astronomy to know full well that what he is seeing is hugely distant from him, both in space and in time, because of the time it takes for light to travel all the way to his eye. Within himself, at that moment, he may well feel that he is at the centre of the universe. But if another 'I' on that same star were to look for him at the very same moment, he would not yet even exist for his observer, since the light carrying information about his existence would only just be starting its long journey.

As Buddha was saying in the Second Noble Truth, an irreducible 'self' or fixed personality cannot logically exist, for it too is part of the universe's relativity – its constant change, or 'becoming'. Thus the ego, generally perceived as the source of consciousness, is in reality a false construct, a fiction designed to cloak its own inherent instability. This Buddhist doctrine of *anatta* (no self) is the third aspect of *dukkha*; and *dukkha, anicca* (impermanence) and *anatta* are together called the three marks in the Sutras, or the fundamental characteristics of existence.

Given all this, however, the question arises: 'If there's no such thing as a self, then what on earth constitutes an individual consciousness or personality?' And Buddha gave his answer through his version of the *skandhas*, the five groups or 'aggregates' of forces and energies that tie us to the world.

1. The Aggregate of Matter. This grouping includes the body, analyzed in terms of four elements (solidity, fluidity, heat and motion) and their derivatives, which include the five sensory organs: eyes, ears, tongue, nose and skin.

2. The Aggregate of Feeling (or Sensation). This grouping includes all sensations that are classified as pleasant, unpleasant or neutral, and arise through the encounter of the physical and mental organs with objects in the world. (The mind or brain is regarded here as one of

these.) They include the creation of visual forms, of sounds, smells, tastes, tactile sensations and – with the addition of mind – ideas, mental images and so on.

3. The Aggregate of Perception. Perception is the faculty which actually recognizes something in the world by picking out its characteristic features and distinguishing it from other things. It arises from the interaction of the sensory organs and the mind with the object in question.

4. The Aggregate of Mental Formations. This grouping includes all mental constructs: volitions and intentions; determination; heedlessness; intuition; and the idea of the self. These constructs also include the three poisons noted earlier: desire, ignorance and aversion. All these things are the raw material of *karma*, because they are the root cause of why and how we act. Mental formations and behaviour, in fact, cannot really be separated, for in a sense they are one and the same thing. As the *Dhamapada*, quoted in Clive Erricker's *Teach Yourself Buddhism* (for which I am grateful for this account of the *skandhas*) explains:

> What we are today comes from our thoughts of yesterday, and our present thoughts build our life of tomorrow. Our life is the creation of our mind.
> If a man speaks or acts with an impure mind, suffering follows him as the wheel of the cart follows the beast that draws the cart . . . If a man speaks or acts with a pure mind, joy follows him as his own shadow.

5. The Aggregate of Consciousness. This is an awareness of all the other four aggregates that supervenes out of their conjunction, *but is*

not – and cannot be – independent of them. 'There is no arising of consciousness without conditions,' said the Buddha to Sati the Fisherman's Son, who saw otherwise. Consciousness, that is to to say, cannot exist separately from the other *skandhas* – and just as they are impermanent, constantly on the move, so must consciousness be. What we perceive as the self, the 'I' – a sort of fixed, central command-centre and immutable point of reference – is, then, an illusion. All 'we' have access to is an impersonal succession of sense-impressions and awarenesses. In their constant flow, these may create a sense of 'identity' as a by-product, because they seem to be happening to 'us'. But the idea of a fixed independent selfhood – or ego – is an ongoing fiction. The Buddha understood how sensations, endlessly following one another, might create the impression of a self which seems to 'possess' the senses which apprehend them, but denied that there was any organizing principle at all 'behind' or 'above' either.

In other words, the raw material out of which we construct the world is nothing more – and *can* be nothing more – than a continual succession of mental and physical phenomena. Each individual is a compound of components, that is to say, which are constantly changing. Clive Erricker in *Teach Yourself Buddhism* gives an example, which is also an example of the *skandhas* in action:

> I am hungry and I am presented with a plate of food. I see it, smell it, and anticipate the taste. I am aware of what is in the dish. Sensations arise and perceptions follow, with the recognition of what it will be like to taste it. Volition is brought into play, I wish to eat. I pick up my knife and fork; all other concerns vanish from my mind as I indulge in the pleasure of eating. As my stomach becomes full, my desire decreases. My mind turns to other things. New sensations,

perceptions and mental formations arise. I am more interested in my partner's conversation, dwell on the discomfort in my stomach. I wish to do other things. I suggest it is time to leave. I look forward to what happens next, or I view it with disappointment – the end of an enjoyable evening and a new working day. I am enveloped in the never-ending process of continual arising (or 'dependent origination'), a chain of cause and effect that never ceases.

Life, the Buddha taught, does not have to be this way, forever shifting between aversion and desire in a maze of mental images and perceptions and volitions, in the middle of which I somehow confusedly identify something I call 'myself'. Desire and aversion, he said, are two sides of the same coin: the one inevitably leads to the other, and worldly happiness can never be more than a fleeting sensation – with dissatisfaction built into its very core. The only way to escape from this constant see-saw – or vicious circle – is to confront the fact that the 'I' which longs for happiness and ease is precisely the obstacle which stands in the way of obtaining either. Self is, in fact, *dukkha*. Only by giving up self can happiness be truly achieved.

If there is no such thing as self, though, and it is the fate of all individuals to undergo rebirth, what exactly, according to the teachings of the Buddha, is it that is reborn?

Rebirth

The Buddha firmly rejected the idea of eternalism: that is, he denied the prevailing belief that the soul or self somehow survived death intact. If physical form, feelings, perceptions and mental formations were all impermanent, after all, how could the self, which was merely their by-product, be anything more permanent than they were? Even in life, there is no abiding aspect of a person that is solid and unchanging enough to house what we call a self. When that person dies, therefore – and the other four *skandhas* pass away – there simply cannot be any residue or leftovers to pass on.

At the same time, though, the Buddha also rejected eternalism's metaphysical opposite – so-called annihilationism. That is, the idea that when a person dies, 'bang, that's that' – there is no afterlife at all. For that would have been to accept that human life lacks all meaning and purpose – and under those circumstances it wouldn't matter how anyone behaved, for there would be nothing to lose. Hedonism – total abandonment to every passing lust or caprice – would be the order of every day. Yet the Buddha saw this option as bringing about the worst possible of all conditions. Why? The answer lies in *karma*, a concept which is absolutely central to Buddhist ethics and to Buddha's teachings on the matter of rebirth.

Karma

Put at its simplest, *karma* is the law of cause and effect. It says that anything at all that happens has been caused by something else, and in turn causes other things. All living things are links in this continuous chain of cause and effect – births and deaths are simply small events in an endless cycle. Birth brings the *skandhas* together into a particular formation and death dissipates them again, but past actions and intentions – including those we 'ourselves' have injected (or will inject) into the stream – continue to play themselves out, rolling on regardless. *Karma*, therefore, should be understood as being – at one and the same time – what 'we' inherit from the past and what 'we' contribute to the future.

In the West, the word *karma* has had a bad press – it has been assumed that it refers to a deterministic and fatalistic view of life, or to some immutable destiny that we can do nothing to alter. But the Buddhic idea of *karma* – the on-rolling tide of cause and effect – is a great deal more than that. Yes, it is used in Buddhism to explain the differing conditions of people in the world – past good or bad deeds in other lives being responsible for their station or position in this one. And yes, it is used to help explain mass deaths and disasters (collective *karma*). But that is only because the law of *karma* decrees that everything *must* have a cause, even if it lies outside our ability to grasp it – this rule lies right at the heart of Buddhist ethics. It is not only the answer to everything-that-is, but also to the essential question of morality, which is 'Why should we be good'? *Because what we do and how we act produces personal, communal, human and spiritual consequences.*

One can see this principle at work on a personal level without any difficulty. For it is a truism that what we do has consequences which profoundly affect how we feel and what subsequently happens to us. A sudden outburst of anger, for example, can sour relations with others for hours, days or weeks – it might even be the cause of a permanent break and either leave us guilt-ridden or full of a defensive (or crowing) self-justification. ('Losing my temper was both right and effective; in the same circumstances I'd do it – even use it as a tactic – again.') Equally, a sudden moral lapse can have truly devastating consequences, such as the loss of a fortune or a career.

It is not only the bad things we do, however, that produce an effect. It would be a mistake if we only laid stress on the effect of so-called 'bad' karma, which in the traditional view may lead to rebirth as a poor or sickly person, an animal or an insect, or even an occupant, for aeons of time, of one of the Buddhist hells. That way lies guilt and terror of life. The Buddhist monk Ajahn Sumedho, quoted in John Snelling's *The Buddhist Handbook*, explains:

> We worry: 'I've done so many bad things in the past; what kind of result will I get from all that?' Well, all you can know is what you've done in the past is a memory now. The most awful, disgusting thing that you've ever done, that you wouldn't want anyone to know about; the one that, whenever anyone talks about karma and rebirth, makes you think, 'I'm really going to get it for having done that' – that is a memory, and that memory is the karmic result. The additions to that like fearing, worrying, speculating – these are the karmic result of unenlightened behaviour. What you do, you remember; it's as simple as that. If you do something kind, generous or compassionate, the memory makes you feel happy; and if you do something mean and nasty, you have to remember *that*. You try to repress it, run away from it, get caught up in all kinds of frantic behaviour – that's the karmic result.

Sumedho goes on to say that the only way to get rid of this sort of karmic result – or karmic formation, as it is often called – is to confront and recognize it fully. In meditation, karmic formations are encouraged to rise into the mind and then to disappear and die – without being acted upon, stresses Snelling. For whenever a karmic formation is acted upon in any way – good or bad – its life is prolonged and its power is increased. Habits of mind and behaviour that become harder and harder to break out of are created little by little.

Since breaking out – escaping from an endlessly reduplicated state of ignorance and *angst* – was absolutely central to the Buddha's mission to humanity, *karma* also plays a fundamental role, for it represents a demonstration-in-action of the practicability of his insight. Ethical considerations are paramount, because liberating oneself from the realm of *samsara* is ultimately a karmic matter, one that is rooted in our everyday activities and behaviour. We are not, that is to say, merely the passive prisoners of our past and of our karmic inheritance, but we have free will and the freedom to act in ways that can and will counter the burden of *karma* we carry. By freely and intentionally choosing how to behave, in other words, we can opt either to improve our lives or call down future misery upon ourselves. Living an ethical (or unethical, careless) life will alter the conditions of our rebirth through the *karma* it generates. Any conduct that lessens attachment to the physical world will lessen desires and lead to a better existence when the wheel turns next time, but if we remain wilfully ignorant of this fact and subject ourselves to oblivious craving, we will turn out to have been our own worst enemies both in this and future lives.

Karma, responsibility for one's own actions and the prospect of rebirth, then, are intimately tied together into a single system. They are the three great pillars that support the Buddhic insistence on the importance of ethics. For if rebirth – which is axiomatic for Buddhists since it was seen and experienced directly by the Buddha – were to be removed from this triad, then though it would still be possible to conduct oneself morally, the morality would be a narrow one and the idea of *karma* would be reduced to the level of a philosophy, a way of explaining, predicting and improving our own and others' behaviour. It is the prospect of rebirth, however, that ultimately buttresses Buddhist ethics and gives Buddha's message real purchase, for once we recognize that our ignorance and craving have consequences and the state of affairs that produces them in us goes on forever, the value of happiness and creature comforts as an alternative to living ethically takes a very sharp nose-dive indeed.

What is the point, after all, of a present, relatively comfortable existence if the struggle has to continue lifetime after lifetime with no escape except by your own efforts? What does it matter that the cell in which you're currently serving time is comfortable enough if you're permanently condemned to the prison of *samsara*? Something must be done, and it must be done now. It's 'your' responsibility to 'yourself' and to the whole world of creation. It's a matter – literally – of life and death.

Why, though? And here we have to return to the question we started out with: if the self is impermanent, what exactly is it that is reborn, and what relation does it have to the life being led now? What Buddha said was that although there was no transmigration between the lives of palpable selves or souls, there was still *a causal connection* between one life and another. The karmic accumulations of a particular life – itself the end-product of endless numbers of previous causally-linked lives – condition in their turn a new birth. Sequences of lives interconnected in this way form a continuum, though nothing is passed on but the conditioning, the karmic charge.

Put another way, our past actions and intentions continue to play themselves out even when the characteristics 'responsible' for them has disappeared. The good or bad *karma* accumulated then flows into a new set of characteristics which will neither be the same as the old one, nor completely different; its form and nature will depend on the quality of the unexpended *karma* which remained when the previous set died or disintegrated. The energy of this karma, not yet dissipated, will continue to play itself out in a new life.

The concept of rebirth without identity was, the Buddha knew, a hard one to grasp, so he drew an analogy with a drop of water taken from a great river. The drop, once extracted, seems to have a separate 'life' or identity of its own. Later, though, it is returned to the river and a second drop is taken, and although this second drop is made from exactly the same constituents as the first, there is no continuity of identity between it or any other drops.

Other metaphors have come to be used for this reconstitution of elements without the identicalness of a transferred eternal 'self'. One is of a flame that is passed from candle to candle. It is not exactly the same flame that is passed down the line, but it is not exactly a different one either. Another example comes from the cannoning of billiard or pool balls. The first ball hits a second and stops dead; the second ball hits a third and does the same; but the third ball continues. A single charge of kinetic energy, in other words, passes through a number of temporary vehicles.

Dependent Origination

Linked to *karma* – and, in a sense, indivisible from it in Buddhic thought – the great rolling tide of cause and effect is what is called the doctrine of dependent origination (*Paticassamuppada*). Buddhism does not (unlike Hinduism, for instance) acknowledge the existence of a creator god; and Buddha himself made it clear that nothing in the world is self-creating. His disciples, then, needed to know how and why phenomena came into existence at all under these circumstances. Also, where did cause and effect emerge from and why did some things seem to be eternal and uncaused – to have a 'life' of their own – while others seemed to leave no trace after being extinguished?

Buddha explained this in terms of a closed system of causal links – a circle of causes and effects that inevitably leads back to its own starting point in order to kick-start the chain reaction once more. There are (according to the usual interpretation) twelve elements or stages in this self-generating and self-perpetuating loop:

1. *Ignorance.* This is the state we are born into when we enter the wheel of becoming. It is the root cause of our false sense of self, our separation from the world and our desperate clinging to life. For ignorance leads to

2. *Will-to-Action.* Innate tendencies arise which lead all sentient creatures to act intentionally in a particular way, either good or bad. Will-to-action gives rise to

3. *Consciousness,* which in turn leads to

4. *Name and Form.* Without consciousness, or a sense of 'self', there would be no objects for us to find ourselves relative to. An object is meaningless, inert, without a subject to perceive and apprehend it. Name and form might be called psycho-physical interaction between an organism and the world, and it leads to the creation of

5. *The Six Bases.* These are the five senses and the mind; and they in turn give rise to

6. *Sense-impressions (or Contact).* This is the information about the world derived from sight, smell, hearing, taste, touch and the activity of the mind; and it causes

7. *Feelings.* From feelings (or emotions) come

8. *Attachment.* Attachments to things and ideas in the world are created by a desire which can never fully be satisfied. The organism clings to these attachments – to objects, ideas, ideals – and experiences suffering, which in turn condemns it to

9. *Being or Becoming,* the inevitable result of which is

10. *Rebirth.* Rebirth – being born at all – leads to

11. *Ageing and Death.* And ageing and death – the whole sorrowful experience of living – leads back once more, unless intervened in, to the beginning of the circle of dependent origination in ignorance. One life-cycle thus inevitably leads to another – and so on and on through vast aeons of time. This is 'the fearful cosmic roundabout', to borrow John Snelling's memorable phrase, to which we are all doomed – unless we do something about it.

The Wheel of Becoming

The entire realm of *samsara*, as described in the first two of Buddha's Four Noble Truths, is pictured in what is called the Wheel of Becoming. The wheel is clamped in the jaws of Yama, the Lord of Death, a dragon-like figure with three eyes, fangs and a crown of skulls, and its outer rim is an aide-memoire for the doctrine of dependent origination. The figure at the top is a blind man, representing ignorance, the inability to see. Moving clockwise, there follows a potter, representing the will-to-action of the potter's wheel, and a monkey, who stands for the constant restlessness of undirected consciousness. Next are three men in a boat – the boat of karmic inheritance – being carried across a stream towards interaction with the world of living things, and houses with doors and windows, which represent the opening of the doors of the six senses that let that world in.

The image of the lovers which follows symbolizes the contact between these senses and objects in the world that results in sense-impressions, and the man with an arrow in his eye stands for the fact that the feelings aroused by this contact are often so strong that they partially blind us – we lose sight of the way and stumble into desire. The man drinking, who is next, depicts the continuous craving (or thirst) that this produces, and the monkey clinging to a fruit tree (for dear life) illustrates the slavish attachment to objects of desire (and/or aversion) that are formed in life as a result. The inevitable outcome of this attachment is the pregnant woman who follows – a new embryo, condemned to becoming, has been formed, and when it is born into the world from the woman giving birth, who is next, it is doomed to decay over time into the last image of all, an old man carrying a corpse. The corpse-carrier, directly beneath the jaws of Yama, is carrying his burden towards a lake – perhaps representing death, the dissolution of the body – from which the blind man, under the same jaws, seems to have just stepped. The long carousel of life and death, then, continues to whirl on without stopping.

At the centre of the wheel, its controlling hub, are three animals: a pig, a snake and a cock. These, sometimes known as the Three Poisons or the Three Fires, are the vices which keep the world of *samsara* spinning on its axis. The pig is ignorance (unawareness, delusion); the snake is hatred (anger, aggression, violence); and the cock is greed (craving, lust, unslaked desire). In a circle of their own, they are shown as swallowing each other's tails (or else spewing each other up) in yet another endless and continuous cycle – the implication of which is that any one of them can and does generate the next, and that the energy created and expended in their hectic pursuit (or creation) of each other both powers the spinning world and is 'self'-consuming.

(This – as a psychological insight – is clear enough, for ignorance of the way in which the world turns encourages us to believe that the fulfilment of our desires will lead to enduring happiness, at no cost to ourselves. Realizing that this is not so, in the end, can have extreme reactive consequences, as can failing to get what we want in the first place. In turn, anger, by its nature, leads to the perpetuation of ignorance and desire can result in violence. They really do belong, all three of them, in the same dog-eat-dog spin.)

Surrounding the wheel's energetic hub is another circular domain, which is divided into two equal sectors, sometimes distinguished by their black and white colouring. In one half (white), figures are seen climbing upwards; in the other (black), they are descending towards free fall. This represents the karmic movement of all organisms, which are either intent on struggling upwards to a higher state of being or descending willy-nilly to a lower existence under the gravitational pull of illusion. The fact that this vignette is also circular and continuous means that those who climb will sooner or later fall; those who fall will 'survive' to climb once again, and so on and so on, to use Shakespeare's phrase in *Macbeth*, 'to the last syllable of recorded time'.

The remainder of the wheel between the central circles and the surrounding rim is divided by its spokes into (usually) six separate *samsaric* realms into which rebirth is possible. At the top are the gods (*devas*) in paradise, a place of pleasure and ease. To their right is the realm of the titans (jealous gods, *asuras*) who are constantly doing battle in an attempt to reach the top spot. (A tree that grows out of their realm provides fruit for the gods above, and a titan is shown trying to chop the tree down to get at it: his heart's desire.) The three sectors below this are the three lower realms: those of animals, of the damned suffering purgatory and of the so-called hungry ghosts (or *pretas*). These ghosts haunt the earth in a permanent state of hunger and thirst, but can never take in enough to satisfy their swollen bellies through their scrawny necks and tiny mouths. The small and unnourishing fruits they are competing for are protected by thorns and spiky branches.

The final realm, at the top left of the Wheel – and occupying a central position between the three lower realms and those of the gods and titans – is that of humans conducting their ordinary, everyday lives under the sway of karmic desire and conditioning. They eat, drink and work; they give birth and are treated for sickness; they grow old and die in ignorance with no chance of salvation. The only sign of hope is the presence of two ascetics under a tree, meditatively reflecting on the scenes around them. They are there to show that only in the human realm can virtue and wisdom be increased.

The six realms are a pictorial demonstration of the inevitability of rebirth and of the various conditions in which it can take place. No organism – not even a god – can remain for ever in one realm; every creature – once its karmic reward or punishment has been played out – is doomed to travel successively through all of them. But the realms, as depicted together in the Wheel, are also a sort of mnemonic for the chains which keep every organism locked within the *samsaric* system. In the case of the gods, it is pride which is their besetting sin; for the titans, it is jealousy; for the animals, brutish instincts; for the denizens of hell, pain and fear; for the hungry ghosts, the constant gnawing of appetite. As for humans, who ought to know better and have the greatest chance of release, it is self-preoccupation – obsessional concern with their ordinary daily lives – that prevents them from seeing clearly. This is the mirror that Yama holds up to us, a mirror in which we can not only see our own fate but also the drives, traps and delusions that keep us tied to the Wheel.

There is, however, one further figure featured in the ikon – and that is the Buddha himself, pictured within a circle, sometimes in each one of the *samsaric* realms, and sometimes standing outside the

Wheel, pointing away from it in another direction. His presence is there to indicate that although the Wheel may represent life-as-it-is, there is still a way to break out of the circle, a way he first outlined for the ascetics in the Deer Park at Sarnath in his Third and Fourth Noble Truths.

The Third Noble Truth: The Cessation of Suffering

If the Third Noble Truth had not been enunciated by Buddha, all he would have left us would be a metaphysical description of the world-as-illness: a collection of syndromes – and a bleak diagnosis – still in search of a cure. What he held out in the Third Truth, however, was the fact that the chronic, everlasting illness of *dukkha* could be treated. He invited all individuals – *so long as they recognized the truth of the disease* – to become, in effect, their own doctors and treat themselves. There was, in other words, a means of escape from *samsara*.

> Bhikkhus [monks], there is an unborn, unoriginated, unmade and unconditioned. Were there not the unborn, unoriginated, unmade and unconditioned, there would be no escape from the born, originated, made and conditioned. Since there is the unborn, unoriginated, unmade and unconditioned, there is escape from the born, originated, made and conditioned.

The key to this escape, he said, lay in control (*nirodha*): control over the craving or thirst (*tanha*) for attachment. If attachment was first rooted out, he went on, then the thirst itself would be extinguished. Once that had been done, a state of *nirvana* could be reached, a state in which there would be no further suffering.

For many people, one of the problems when confronting the prospect of this treatment is with the Buddhic conception of *nirvana*. Although it is clearly a condition in which something very important has been achieved, there is little description in Buddha's teachings of what it is actually like. Buddhists say this is of no importance: what *is* important is simply to begin the treatment as soon as you can. Once you have been offered a cure, after all, for an apparently incurable disease, it is absurd to demand to know first what it will feel like when it has been successful. If it cures you, they say, you will simply know for yourself that you are well, because the suffering and *angst* that is *dukkha* will have come to an end. *Nirvana*, then, is described only metaphorically: it has been variously illustrated as the laying down of an immense load, freedom from prison or, more disturbingly, in the famous *Fire Sermon*, as a last-minute escape from conflagration:

> Bhikkhus [monks], all is burning. And what is the all that is burning? Bhikkhus, the eye is burning, visible forms are burning, visual consciousness is burning, visual impression is burning, also whatever sensation, pleasant or painful or neither-pleasant-nor-painful, arises on account of the visual impression, that too is burning. Burning with what? Burning with the fire of lust, with the fire of hate, with the fire of delusion; I say it is burning with birth, ageing and death, with sorrows, with lamentations, with pains, with griefs, with despairs.

The reason why Buddha consistently discouraged questions into the true nature of *nirvana*, one might imagine, was that any answer he might have given would inevitably have been seen as definitive. All it would have achieved would have been the setting-up of expectations in the minds of his disciples. Expectations, in the Buddhic scheme, create attachments; and these would be just another burden that those who chose to follow his path would have to lay down. He knew, therefore, that any attempt to describe *nirvana* would be doomed to failure, just as Albert Einstein did when asked to explain his theory of relativity in a few words on his first arrival in America. 'Madam', Einstein is reported to have said:

> Two men, one of them blind, were walking down a long and dusty road, and the man who could see said, 'God, what I wouldn't give for a glass of milk!' And the blind man said, 'Glass I know. But what is this milk you speak of?' And the man who could see said, 'Milk is a white liquid'. And the man who was blind said, 'Liquid I know. But what is this white you speak of?' And the man who could see said, 'White is the colour of a swan's feathers'. And the man who was blind said, 'Feathers I know. But what is this swan you speak of?' The man who could see said, 'A swan is, um, well, a bird with a crooked neck.' And the blind man, persisting, said, 'Bird I know, and neck I know. But what is this crooked you speak of?' Finally, in exasperation, the man who could see took the blind man's arm and pulled it out straight from his shoulder. 'That,' he said, 'is straight.' Then he bent it at the elbow. 'And that,' he said, 'is crooked.' And the blind man breathed a sigh and said, 'Ah, now I understand what milk is!'

Nirvana, according to the Buddha's teachings, is equally far beyond the reach of ordinary language and experience. It cannot be described verbally, because words would only limit it. It has to be apprehended directly. In fact, one can only say what it is not. It is not, for example, some form of 'nothingness', for that would be to fall into the trap of annihilationism (complete non-existence) which the Buddha rejected, just as he rejected the possibility of any form of eternal life. It is not, equally, some sort of heaven to which good Buddhists go. For heaven (*svarga*) is merely, in Buddhic thought, another part of *samsara* ('that which goes round forever'). No, the Buddha made it plain that it can only occur in *worldly* conditions and, in the case of humans, within the human body:

> In this fathom-long body, with all its perceptions and thoughts, do I proclaim the world, the origin of the world [and] the cessation of the world . . .

Perhaps *nirvana* is best thought of, first of all, as a state of letting-go: letting go of all false beliefs, all illusions of permanence, any idea of the existence of the self as a fixed point of view. The 'self' disappears and the angle of the devotee's vision becomes universal rather than limited and particular. Thus an individual who now sees the world panoptically – as it is, in and of itself – can act disinterestedly, without any desire for a particular result and without identifying a 'self' in action. Indeed, in the words of Gillian Stokes in her excellent *Buddha: A Beginner's Guide*, 'Such a person knows that there is no self who is the doer or who can die . . . Psycho-physical death cannot touch the person who achieves *nirvana*, because such a person dies to each moment.'

Put another way, then, *nirvana* is transcendence: transcendence beyond the either-or categories of 'existence' and 'non-existence', and the finite, worldly contraries of suffering and happiness, misery and bliss. What is attained is a condition of perfect felicity, a condition that was enshrined in the life and disposition of Buddha and his liberated disciples, according to the *Dhammapada*:

Let us live happily, hating none in the midst of men who hate. Let us live happily, then, free from disease. Let us live happily, then, free from care. Let us live happily, then, we who possess nothing. Let us dwell feeding on joy like the Radiant Gods.

The Fourth Noble Truth: The Path to the Cessation of Suffering

The Fourth Noble Truth, as enunciated by Buddha, represents the practical steps that have to be taken if our inveterate thirst or craving for attachment (*tanha*) is finally to be eliminated – and the ground is to be made fertile for the attainment of *nirvana*. It takes the form of what is known as the Holy or Noble Eightfold Path: eight groups of attributes and/or modes of mental and behavioural conduct, which will help lead his disciples to their final goal. They are:

1. Right Understanding
2. Right Orientation or Thought
3. Right Speech
4. Right Action
5. Right Livelihood
6. Right Effort
7. Right Mindfulness
8. Right Concentration

These are generally construed as covering three main areas. Right Understanding and Thought come under the heading of wisdom, or *prajna*. Right Speech, Action and Livelihood cover the ethical or moral behaviour (*sila*) that is essential for any aspirant; and Right Effort, Mindfulness and Concentration must be deployed in the mental discipline of meditation (*samadhi*), when practised in the correct way.

The Path should not be interpreted as a hierarchical structure of some sort, however – for all its lay-out and division as a spiritual ladder with eight ascending steps. Buddha made it clear that its three main elements (wisdom, ethical behaviour and mental discipline/meditation) had to be developed in concert. Ethical conduct was as necessary to the getting of wisdom as wisdom was to the achievement and interpretation of meditational states. Without the mental discipline of meditation, both a considered moral life and wisdom would remain out of reach.

Ethical Conduct

The importance of a life led ethically has always been at the heart of Buddhic teaching. It is not, however, regarded as an end in itself, but as a means of developing compassion and lessening the amount of suffering in the world, both one's own and that of others. It represents a determination on the part of an individual to help solve the problem of *samsara* at its root by both taking personal responsibility for it and contributing as little as is humanly possible to the world of karmic conditioning. Humility – the abasement of self and the recognition of mistakes – is crucial to this. So are loving kindness, generosity and forgiveness, for by cultivating these things, the individual can keep the damaging reverberations of his or her behaviour – its fall-out – to a minimum.

Right Speech is a necessary part of this karmic self-disarmament, for it involves the avoidance of anything and everything that might take the speaker in harmful directions: swearing, gossiping, backbiting, slandering and wasting other people's time with idle chatter. It also means telling the truth at all times and keeping silent rather than saying something that is neither productive nor helpful.

81

Right Action is aimed, equally, at spiking the guns and defusing the karmic consequences of behaviour – especially unconsidered behaviour. It promotes peaceful and harmonious conduct at all times, and acknowledges that harm done to others represents both personal damage and an out-rippling echo of destruction in the general scheme of things. Certainly, then, one should not take life, nor steal nor immorally appropriate what belongs to other organisms, but one should also not misuse one's own senses by over-indulging in food, or beautiful sights and sounds, or intellectual pastimes. Intoxicants should be avoided at all times. Celibacy, though not mandatory in lay members, was essential to monks pursuing the Path, for an even tenor of mind without distraction and external embroilment – the Middle Way between indulgence and asceticism, according to Buddha's teachings – was the key.

Right Livelihood is a generalized injunction not to practise any trade at all that is in any way harmful to living things, and is in a sense inapplicable to ordained monks and nuns, since they have already embraced it. In the Buddha's own time, its application would have been fairly limited: to butchers, perhaps; soldiers; makers of or dealers in weapons and intoxicants; bandits; thieves; and those who lived by deception. (Now the net, of course, would spread much wider.) But it also represents an encouragement to Buddhists to take up callings, professions or trades that actively promote good and counter the playing-out of karmic conditioning in wars, violence, illness or damage to the environment. Again this is to do with the taking of personal responsibility, and with the recognition that these things have their roots in *dukkha* – to which *sila* (the ethical life) is in the end the only collective antidote. Buddha taught that *sila* is a vital stepping-stone in the path towards felicity and release and this was also recognized by aspirants.

Mental Discipline/Meditation

Meditation, in the words of John Snelling in his book *The Buddhist Handbook*, is:

> the specialized activity that helps us to fully realize the Buddha's teachings – to make them an integral part of our being rather than just a new set of ideas to be entertained theoretically in the mind. It weans [us] away from out usual habit patterns, particularly our involvement with our thoughts and their emotional sub-themes. At the same time it sharpens and intensifies our powers of direct perception: it gives us eyes to see into the true nature of things. The field of research is ourselves, and for this reason the laser of attention is turned and focused inwards.

In this context, *Right Effort* means making the effort to apply oneself conscientiously to the task ahead and to be awake and aware at every moment; to prevent wrong states of mind from arising and/or to dispel them; and to focus only on wholesome and useful states of mind. This requires an act of will, a decision to remain single-minded, for being single-minded is the only way to conquer laziness, doubt, faint-heartedness and the swarming-in of extraneous thoughts and sensations.

Right Mindfulness is to do with application to the here-and-now, to immediate states of consciousness. It involves careful awareness of the activities of the body, and the movements of the mind. It is the watcher, the overseer, of what is going on, the director of Right Effort – with which it is interdependent and co-reliant. Without Effort it would have nothing to produce – just as without Mindfulness, Effort would be random and lead nowhere. Both

Mindfulness and Effort, it should be noted, are not – and should not be – qualities just reserved for the inward examination of the meditation cushion. They are also fundamental to living ethically.

Wisdom

The essential ground-base of wisdom, as outlined by the Buddha, is *Right Understanding*. Anyone who wishes to follow Buddha's Path, in other words, must first have become familiar with his teachings – and have understood them correctly, both in theory and in practice. Any commitment that is made, then, is based on informed confidence in his teachings rather than on blind faith or any superficial attraction. *Right Understanding* is, therefore, the essential background to all other aspects of the Path – the ultimate motivator, for example, of Right Effort.

Right Thought or *Orientation* involves the necessary switch that has to take place in our patterns of thought if we are to reach towards the elimination of self and see the world panoptically. We have literally to reform our minds in order to escape from our periscope-like blinkeredness. We must learn to adopt *other*-directed modes of thought and to understand that the Path is not being followed for any reason of self-advancement but in order to move away from our egocentric world-view and towards self-obliteration – to be reached by the practice of the Path as a whole.

Wisdom, the combination of Right Understanding and Right Thought or Orientation, can be – and often is – seen as the culmination of the Path, its ultimate goal. Its acquisition is gradual and cumulative, though, and it requires overall mental development (*bhavana*). It demands commitment, absolute awareness in the form of meditation and expression that reaches outwards into the world in the form of action. Different schools of Buddhic thought have laid emphasis on one or another of these elements, but have universally agreed on the importance of all three.

The Eightfold Path, then, does not represent any sort of separation of approaches to *nirvana*. It is merely the teasing-out into categories of an all-at-once, directed passage towards final truth. This truth – the end-result of the Path – was described by Buddha to his faithful servant and cousin Ananda shortly before his death:

> Those who have died after the complete destruction of the three bonds of lust, of covetousness, and of the egotistical cleaving to existence, need not fear the state after death. They will not be in a state of suffering; their minds will not continue as a Karma of evil deeds or sin, but are assured of final deliverance. When they die, nothing will remain of them but their good thoughts, their righteous acts, and the bliss that proceeds from truth and righteousness. As rivers must at last reach the distant main, so their minds will be reborn in higher states of existence and continue to press on to their ultimate goal, which is the ocean of truth, the eternal peace of Nirvana.

The Five Hindrances

Elsewere in his teaching, as recorded in the Canon, the Buddha listed the major obstacles to progress that any committed follower would have to confront during his or her journey on the Eightfold Path.

1. Sensual desire
2. Ill will or aversion
3. Sloth or torpor

4. Restlessness and worry
5. Doubt

Sensual desire - with its drive towards attachment - is obviously the enemy of total commitment and concentration, as is *ill will or aversion*. But there are antidotes. Meditation, for example, can be directed towards the more repulsive aspects of the body and conscious good will towards the antipathetic person or object in question, in a way similar to Jesus's admonition to 'love your enemy'. *Sloth or torpor* can also be counteracted, this time by awareness and by the conscious monitoring of the body's intake and activities (what we would now call 'diet' and 'exercise').

Restlessness and worry, for their part, are seen as stemming essentially from a clinging to, and preoccupation with, past misdeeds. This preoccupation can usually be cured by confession and repentance and by a firm resolution never to repeat the misdeeds. A more chronic and persistent form of the obstacle (commonly held to be ubiquitous in the modern world) is simply a sign that the devotee has not yet begun to shake off the shackles that tie him to illusion and to the idea of 'self'. It can only be gradually laid to rest by the experience of the Eightfold Path itself.

The cause of the last of the Hindrances, *Doubt* – dithering and vacillation rather than healthy scepticism – was seen as being incomplete familiarity with the Buddha's teachings. This could be counteracted by further study, by a fuller commitment to the *Dharma* and by talking the matter through with those already on the Path. Guides such as as meditation-monitors, teachers and advisers on conduct were, and have always been, of central importance in Buddhism. It takes two, at the very least, to reach salvation – except, of course, in the case of Buddhas.

Buddhas and the Ordering of Enlightenment

Only Buddhas – fully 'enlightened' or 'awakened' ones – can arrive at Enlightenment without receiving the gift of the *Dharma* from another person and even they, according to a doctrine that emerged after the lifetime of Sakyamuni, have received it many lives previously from a former Buddha (generally believed to appear once every 320,000 years). No-one but Buddhas, in other words, can work out personal salvation unaided. As the *Dhammapada* says:

> You yourself must make an effort. The Buddhas, for their
> part, are the revealers.

Making this effort and following the Eightfold Path may at last bring the initiate a first glimpse of *nirvana*, in which case he or she, according to the Buddha, leaves the ranks of ordinary mortals to become a stream-winner, or *sotapanna*. It would take a stream-winner – one who has 'won' contact with the Path – only seven lifetimes, he said, to reach fully-achieved Enlightenment. At later stages of the Path there were also a variety of saints-to-be – known as once-returners (*sakadagami*) and never-returners (*anagami*) – as well as the saints (or worthy ones, *arhants*) themselves.

Arhants, of whom there were many, it seems, during Gautama Buddha's own lifetime – perhaps because of their earlier experiences as ascetics and seekers – are those who have finally thrown off, once and for all, the so-called 'binding influences' of sensual desire, the desire to exist, wrong views and ignorance. No longer producers of new karmic formations, they persist in the world because old ones still have to be worked out, and they spend what remains of their time teaching the *Dharma*.

Part One: Buddhism in the Time of Buddha

To achieve arhantship, an enlightened teacher is necessary. This is not true of a so-called *pacceka buddha*, a solitary devotee of the Way who achieves Enlightenment alone, but does not teach. The Buddha combined in himself the qualities of both a *pacceka buddha* and an *arhant* – in as much as he achieved Enlightenment alone and went on to teach the *Dharma* – and therefore stands above both.

The last in the hierarchy of those who have glimpsed or achieved *nirvana* is the *Bodhisattva*, or Buddha-to-be – as Gautama Buddha was when he entered his mother's womb in the shape of a white elephant. The process of becoming a Buddha takes immense numbers of lifetimes, during which the *Bodhisattva* is reborn to and remains in the world, not because of any outstanding karmic debts, but due to the sheer force generated by the compassion of the decision to free all organisms from *dukkha*. Later, as we shall see, the concept of the *Bodhisattva* became increasingly important as Buddhism developed.

The Ordained and the Secular in the Buddhic Community

The oldest documents in the Buddhist Canon – generally recognized as originating from the period soon after the Buddha's death – relate to monastic discipline (*vinaya*). One document, the *Skandhaka*, which probably dates back to the fourth century BC, lays out the basic institutions of monastic life: the ceremonies of admission and confession, the rules governing retreats and punishments, clothing, food and the use of medicines. Another, the *Pratimoshka* – which is almost certainly even older – contains a list of two hundred and fifty ecclesiastical offences and it provides an insight into the *Sangha*, or community, which Buddha created and left behind him.

At first – as I have indicated elsewhere – all those entering the community simply had to swear to the Five Precepts. They had to promise that they would:

- avoid harming any living thing
- avoid taking anything not freely given
- forsake the pursuit of sensual pleasures and be celibate
- speak and think truthfully, kindly and compassionately
- avoid all intoxicants

These rules applied to monks, nuns and lay people alike, except that lay people were not required to be chaste – they simply had to avoid both excessive sex and adultery.

Later the Five Precepts were doubled to Ten, and all ordained monks and nuns were enjoined to follow them. Solemn promises were now made to:

- avoid eating solid foods after midday
- avoid frivolous entertainments, such as dancing, singing, music and mime
- avoid perfumes, garlands, jewellery and other personal adornment
- avoid using high seats or beds
- avoid handling gold and silver and all forms of trading

By the time the recitation of the *Pratimoshka* took on its present written form – it has to be recited once a fortnight before a chapter of monks – huge number of sub-clauses had been added to the Ten Precepts and the punishment of infractions was severe. The first four offences – sexual intercourse, theft, murder and false claims, either to supernatural powers or high spiritual attainment – warranted immediate expulsion. The next thirteen – relating to sexual misconduct, creating dissension within the order and building personal huts – deserved suspension. Two sexual offences followed that were punishable according to the circumstances, and thirty other offences resulted in the forfeiture of the right to wear clothing belonging to the order – and made the offender, moreover, liable to an unfavourable rebirth. These particular transgressions of the monastic code included the handling of gold and silver, engaging in trade and appropriating goods intended for the community for personal use.

The next ninety infractions were also punishable by an unfavourable rebirth, unless repented and atoned for. They involved such offences as telling lies or slandering or mocking other monks and they also covered relations with the lay community. Further offences included teaching the Buddha's scriptures word for word to any unordained person and gossiping to lay people about offences committed by monks. The remaining offences added up to an extraordinarily motley collection of misdemeanours which included, among other things, destroying vegetation, digging in the earth, drinking alcohol and possessing a bed or chair with legs more than eight inches high! There were also rules governing correct behaviour and the settling of disputes.

These rules were all introduced, of course, to promote the protection of other living creatures and to provide the best possible conditions for meditation and withdrawal from the everyday nagging temptation of attachment. The frugality and simplicity imposed on the monks was designed to foster their independence, as was their necessary separation from the ties of property, clan and family. In the Buddha's time, the order might well have been composed of no more than wandering mendicants, beggars for alms, who lived in forests or caves away from the towns and villages, feeding and dressing themselves as best they could. They were, however, required by the

Buddha to come together during the rainy season, and out of this practice, no doubt, developed the first monasteries. As the *Sangha* became richer, these monastic foundations spread and remaining together year-round became, at the same time, an increasingly practical option for the ordained monks and nuns. Not only did it sustain their necessary separation from social concerns without the daily rigours of a hand-to-mouth existence, but it also gave them a permanent presence among a lay community which, from then on, became not only their congregation but also their providers.

What was the relationship of ordained monks and nuns to lay members in the early *Sangha*? The laity, after all, had 'taken refuge' in exactly the same way as the ordained, by proclaiming the Three Jewels and taking up the Five Precepts. It seems that the relationship, from the beginning, was a rather condescending one, for 'visible' and 'invisible' *Sanghas* were distinguished at an early stage. The 'visible' *Sangha* consisted of ordained and lay members alike, but there arose within it an élite, known as the 'true' or 'invisible' *Sangha*, which was made up of the *arhants* ('noble' or 'holy' ones). These were regularly contrasted with ordinary worldlings, who were known as 'the foolish common people' (*bala-prthag-jana*). Since ordained monks, with their yellow robes, were at least on their way to achieving *arhant* status, the lay community was regarded by many of them as belonging, essentially, to another species.

The difference between the two member-classes was built into eartly Buddhist thought, for they were seen (by *arhants* and therefore by monks) as occupying two entirely separate planes of existence, the 'wordly' and the 'supramondane'. Only *arhants* were truly alive, since only they had experienced a spiritual rebirth – they were sufficiently detached from the world of conditioning to approach *nirvana*. 'The foolish common people', on the other hand, were so mired in *samsara* that all they could do was muddle along through life in a state of permanent fuddlement. Once in a while, of course, one of them, through prolonged teaching and meditation, might systematically be able to see worldly objects for what they really were – that is, mere hindrances. By then, though, he or she – now able to apprehend *nirvana* as the ultimate objective – was said by definition to have 'ceased to belong to the common people' and to have become transmogrified into one of 'the family of the *arhants*'.

This early perception of the laity as somehow representing a different order of life – for all its support of monastic communities – later became a matter of some dispute, as we shall see, as Buddhism spread across the whole subcontinent of India. So, too, did a large number of doctrinal points which had seemed so authoritative in the mouth of Buddha and yet appeared to need, once he had died, much further elaboration. It was not long before these doctrinal points caused the Buddhist *Sangha* to split into a number of different sects.

Part Two:
Buddhism after Buddha

Chapter Five:

The First Five Hundred Years

The Scriptures

The Buddha in life had never suggested that he was indispensable, either as a leader or as a canonical authority. Though he preached a doctrine of salvation, he was neither a Caliph nor a Pope and he made no arrangements for his successor. Only his teaching, his *Dharma*, he repeatedly told his disciples, was necessary to those who wished to follow the Path. Soon after his death – according to Buddhist tradition – five hundred of his most senior monks gathered in a cave at Rajagaha to determine what exactly that teaching had been. Their aim was to hammer out an exact account of it, as nearly as they could – an authorized version.

The story goes that one of the monks, Upali, passed on the details, under questioning, of when and under what circumstances the Buddha had laid down each rule that governed the lives of his monks (the *Vinaya*). Although the Buddha had once remarked that the *Sangha* could abolish the minor rules, if it so wished, no-one had actually asked him what these were; so Upali's listing of regulations, both major and minor, effectively passed into scripture. His intimate disciple Ananda then recalled the Buddha's basic teachings, the *Sutras*, as exactly as he could. These were afterwards debated in open session, when a form that was acceptable to a majority of the monks present was finally found.

The story of this conclave may well be a myth, but it reflects what is very likely to have occurred soon after Buddha's death – an attempt to standardize Buddhist teaching and practice at a time when few could read and even fewer could write. Both of the texts that are said to have been discussed at the conclave lie somewhere at the heart of later (written) Buddhist literature. One can easily imagine them being taken back to the scattered communities of the *Sangha* by 'living books' – individual monks who set out to memorize all or part of them in the manner of Ray Bradbury's story *Fahrenheit 451*. They must have been gradually translated into local languages and dialects over the next generation or two: the beginning of a process that saw them transmitted orally within communities, from one monk to another, for fully three, perhaps four, hundred years.

As far as we can gather from the first written texts – recorded some time in the first century BC in what is now Sri Lanka – considerable efforts seem to have been made to maintain their purity during this oral period. Inevitably, however, distortions and local variations crept in, particularly in the record of the Buddha's teachings, which came to combine – as far as the laity were concerned – instruction and village entertainment. Since there was also considerable merit attached to their learning and recitation, the teachings appear to have ballooned at an early stage, not only with mnenonic devices such as strategically-placed repetitions but also with poetic embellishments and rhetorical flourishes. It was perhaps felt that the longer they were spun out, the more benefit was attached to their memorization. Another reason was that their acceptance as a canonical entity had not been universal, so some Buddhist communities (perhaps unrepresented at the conclave) had adopted their own versions.

The *Sutras*, then – to a far greater extent, as it turned out, than the rule-book of the *Vinaya* – gradually gave up their authoritative status as a kind of holy writ and became a burgeoning and spiralling series of descants on Buddhic themes. Within them, of course, there still remained the core of the *Dharma*. However, the idea of some sort of received doctrinal infallibility was abandoned (as the Buddha himself no doubt would have wished, given the *ad hoc* quality of his teachings in life) in favour of a generalized freedom to interpret, at both a communal and an individual level. The ideal of Enlightenment, it came to be widely accepted, could be reached by different roads. It was up to each initiate to find the path that best suited him, among the multiple choices represented in the gathering maze of the existing oral literature, which soon became too vast for a single 'living book' to learn and transmit.

Early Schisms and Sects

Given this latitude of interpretation, it is not surprising that divisions within the *Sangha* appeared – sooner rather than later – nor is it remotely surprising that the first of these divisions involved the relationship between Buddhist monks and the lay community which supported them. The Buddha, as we have seen, had allowed in his teachings that laypersons could – and indeed did – achieve the first three levels of sainthood ('stream-winner', 'once-returner' and 'never-returner'). Whether an ordinary citizen, unbound to the monastic life, could reach the ultimate level and become an *arhant* remained a matter of some dispute – although the *Sutras* in fact list twenty individuals who have done so – and it soon became generally accepted that no mere householder could achieve this, the highest status.

The early monasteries came to be regarded more and more as privileged spiritual hothouses for the propagation and conservation of *arhants*, particularly by the monks who inhabited them. Those accepted as such began to see themselves as achieved embodiments of the true *Dharma*, living at the top of an aspirational pyramid, so that only they could pronounce judgment on matters of doctrine and the holiness of others. As a result, they soon formed a kind of spiritual oligarchy, an oligarchy in which other monks became less and less important and lay people played a walk-on role as obedient provisioners and caterers.

Divisions within the Sangha

According to Buddhist tradition, this drift in the affairs of the *Sangha* came to a head on two occasions in the 150 years or so that followed the death of the Buddha. The first crisis, in about 380 BC, was caused by the relaxation of a number of *Vinaya* rules by the monks of Vaisali, thereby allowing themselves to handle gold and silver (in defiance of the Buddha's instructions). They started to collect money instead of food from the lay community and when one of the monks objected – and even went so far as to tell local villagers (successfully) not to donate – he was suspended for preaching without authorization. A council of eminent monks was convened when he passed this news on to other communities, that both ordered his reinstatement and severely censured the Vaisali monastery for its high-handed, non-Buddhic behaviour.

Another, not dissimilar, dispute arose about forty years later –

this time striking at the power of the *arhants*. A number of propositions began to circulate, designed to undermine their claims to omniscience and their self-proclaimed dissimilarity to other mortals. An *arhant*, after all – these new schismatics pointed out – could still be seduced by another person or in a dream; could doubt; could be ignorant and require teaching; could use human speech as a means to enter the Way; and could even spontaneously utter the word *dukkha* (suffering) while meditating. Of course, this hardly constituted a major bill of attainder, but it was the opening salvo, as it turned out, of what became a war of sorts between the traditionalists, the *Sthaviras* (or Elders) and what came to be known as 'the Great-Assemblyites' (the *Mahasanghikas*).

The Mahasanghikas

Inspired by a Buddhist teacher called Mahadeva, the *Mahasanghikas* regarded the *Dharma* as something more than merely a pathway designed for a limited few who lived in seclusion and were subject to strict rules – their aim was to open it up to ordinary people, to increase the chances of a general salvation. They invited non-*arhant* monks and householders to their gatherings and responded to popular religious concerns, claiming that in doing so they were being far truer to the Buddha's teachings than was the exclusive, high-priest-like bureaucracy of the Elders with its mantle of self-proclaimed orthodoxy.

The *Mahasanghikas* differed from the Elders, too, in their views on the essential nature of the Buddha and it is worth examining these for a moment, since they later fed into a general movement within Buddhism which was to become known as the *Mahayana* ('The Great Vehicle or Course'). They downplayed the Buddha's status as a historical human figure and instead turned him into an object of religious faith: transcendental and supramondane, without imperfections, omniscient, all-powerful and eternal. (The historical Buddha, they maintained, had simply been created by the transcendental Buddha in order for him to be able to appear in the world as a teacher.) At the same time — paradoxically, to some extent – they placed him firmly back into the world as a source of constant aid to suffering beings of every kind. He had in no sense, they said, simply 'disappeared' into *nirvana*. Instead, he was an unsleeping watcher, eternally vigilant, and his boundless compassion continued to reverberate in the world in all sorts of different ways: by means of the messengers he would continue to despatch into all the realms of the world until the end of time and through the manifestations of himself that occupied every corner of the universe.

The *Mahasanghikas*, and those that followed their pathway towards the *Mahayana*, also began to raise what turned out to be increasingly important philosophical questions: about the nature of reality and consciousness, for example; the status of knowledge; and the existence (or non-existence) of the self. They maintained that thought – which might be called consciousness-in-action – was in its essence lucent and pure, but that all impurities within it were adventitious contaminations. In line with their downgrading of *arhants*, they also questioned the value of any and all knowledge that could be expressed verbally or in conceptual form. The world and all worldly things, they announced with varying degrees of passion, belonged to the realm of unreality, so only their total absence – or 'emptiness' – could in the end be described as real. Everything else that was, was not; and nothing that could be said about it referred to anything of substance at all.

The members of another schismatic sect that later ran foul of the Elders continued this line of philosophical exploration, while at the same time trying to bring back into place a rather more commonsense view of the world. These were the so-called *Pudgalavadins* or Personalists, who challenged the received canonical view that the 'self' (*pudgala*) was a fiction which had no place in ultimate reality.

The Personalists

The Personalists maintained instead that the self actually existed – not the sort of self, to be sure, that ignorant people constructed for themselves but one that nonetheless provided a sort of transcendental continuity for the events that 'happened' to an individual over a number of consecutive lives, up to and including Buddhahood.

In this the Personalists were – at least in part – reverting to the concepts of the *atman* (self) and of *brahman* (cosmic essence) that were contained in the Upanishads; and they had to perform a difficult balancing act to be able to accommodate Buddhist dogma concerning "the erroneous belief in the self". They were able to do this by asserting that the personality that survived transmigration on the road to *nirvana* was neither identical with the five *skandhas* that constituted what might be called the personhood of a particular living individual, nor was it different from them. Instead its relationship to them was as fire is to fuel, both identical and different at the same time. If a personality were indeed different from the *skandhas*, after all, it would have to be regarded as eternal and unconditional: if it were the same, it would be subject to annihilation. These alternatives, as they pointed out, were both heretical, for they flew in the face of Buddha's teaching.

The Personalists also used this notion of 'both-at-onceness' to characterize the relationship between the *dharmas* (the phenomenal world) and *nirvana*. Buddhist orthodoxy at the time, as represented by the Elders, held that *nirvana* was an utterly transcendent state, with no roots of any kind in the illusory realm of *samsara*. By contrast, the Personalists argued that if a person is neither the same as nor different from its components (as above), then its cessation must *also* be neither the same nor different. The concepts of the world of illusion and the final leaving of it thus bear a similar (fuel-fire) relationship to each other, just as the personality does to the *skandhas*.

All of this may now seem rather dry and remote, but what the Personalists were seeking was a renewed sense of the importance of life in the world. (They also argued that although both the person and the phenomena that 'happened' to it might be unreal, they neverthless provided a framework onto which both knowledge and mutually comprehensible statements could be hung.) If the realm of the spiritual, after all, exists in an entirely different domain from that of the physical, the profane, then worldly activities can have no spiritual value, unless – and only unless – they contribute to escape from the one into the other. If spirituality, on the other hand, is somehow inherent in the world – as they argued – then worldly, secular activities such as raising a family or conducting scientific or philosophical enquiry can be said to have intrinsic worth. Buddhism, like Christianity, has seesawed between these two positions over the centuries but, like Christianity, it has by and large adopted the Middle Way between them, embracing neither the extreme other-wordliness of the Gnostics, for example, nor the extreme world-centredness of, say, orthodox Judaism.

The Personalists were to go on to become a powerful force

within Buddhism – in the seventh century AD, a traveller called Yuan Tsang estimated that over a quarter of all India's 250,000 monks were Personalists. Another schismatic sect, the so-called All-Is-Ists or *Sarvastivadins*, that appeared about fifty years after the Personalists, also became prominent. Led by a sage called Katyayaniputra, they maintained that things in the world, far from being altogether illusory and impermanent, do in fact exist – and not only in the present, but also in the past and future. They struck yet another blow, that is to say, for a commonsense view of the world and for ordinary experience, both of which appear – to the uninitiated at any rate – to unfold serially.

All-Is-Ists

The re-appraisal of the past and the future was the most significant heterodoxy within the schismatic philosophy of the All-Is-Ists, for this struck right at the heart of Buddhist meditational practices. Central to these practices was the concept of impermanence – each initiate was required to engrave the full significance of impermanence on his mind in order to be able to cancel out the anti-spiritual gravitational drag exerted by worldly things. He had to take an event, or *dharma*, and parse it out into its rise and fall – how it 'comes, becomes, and goes'. This inevitably drew him into questions about the nature of time, of course, and into a consideration of the status of the past and the future. Were both unreal? Did only the present truly exist? And if so, exactly how long did the present last? If it was only for an instant, the generally accepted view, then nothing in the world could exist for any longer: it had to be annihilated and re-created (just like present time) from instant to instant.

This particular All-Is-Ist view not only ran counter to

commonsense intuition – the way in which we collectively experience and negotiate the world – but it also produced considerable difficulties for the Buddhist doctrine of karmic effects. If an event or action in the past had instantaneously passed from the present and had ceased to exist, how could it possibly lead to a reward or punishment many years later? (This would require it to have an effect at a time when it was non-existent.) Furthermore, if both past and future events and actions were non-existent, how could we possibly either have knowledge of the past or be able to make predictions about the future, since both memory and prediction require the presence in the mind of an extant object of thought?

For all their appeal to ordinary experience, these All-Is-Ist views failed to find general acceptance. They were voted down at a Buddhist council held in about 250 BC (according to tradition) and the monks of the All-Is-Ists migrated away from the main body of the *Sangha* to the north and the west, where they established strong centres, particularly in Kashmir. From there, with the help of Indo-Greek kings such as Menander, who is said to have converted to Buddhism – and on the back of successive invasions from Bactria and Parthia – they spread out along the Silk Road between China and the West, before becoming a significant influence on the development of Buddhism in China. They also left behind them on the subcontinent an enduring legacy: the notion of a new type of spiritual hero which was to become of great importance in the *Mahayana*: the *bodhisattva*.

The *bodhisattva*, in contrast to the *arhant* and the (private, non-teaching and non-preaching) *pacheka* buddha – both of whom seek release from the cycle of rebirth for themselves alone – is a fully-achieved spirit who chooses to return again and again to the world of *samsara* in order to help others. It became necessary to practise what are called the six perfections when following the path of the *bodhisattva* (giving; morality; patience; vigour; meditation; and wisdom) and the six perfections are a still reverberating echo of All-Is-Ist doctrine.

This brief account of sects and rifts in the early history of the *Sangha* is necessarily schematic. In fact, Buddhist tradition identifies eighteen different schisms during the two-and-a-half centuries or so after the Buddha's death and it is likely that there have been many more – some caused by rivalry between monks, perhaps, some by genuine philosophical differences. It is best, I think, to imagine a period of often intense debate centering on such central issues as the relationship between the monks and laypeople; the degree to which *arhant*-ship was a fully achieved state or one that was subject to temptation and a fall from grace; the true nature of *nirvana*; the status of worldly experience; and the interrelationships between the concepts of death, determinism and *karma* and death, rebirth and time. There is little evidence of *ukases,* followed by acts of excommunication by some sort of central authority, being issued against heretics – except perhaps in the case of the All-Is-Ists. Instead it seems likely that 'homeless' monks of varying philosophical convictions interacted on a more or less reasonable level and that the debate was spread through the *Sangha* by the constant coming-and-going of mendicant initiates and of monks making pilgrimage or taking part in collective retreat.

The emergence of a new class of canonical literature in the third century BC – the *Abhidharma* – made it much more likely that there was indeed considerable philosophical debate of just this kind about the teachings of the Buddha. The *Abhidharma*, which means 'above or about the *Dharma*', is a systematic teasing-out of key themes and topics that are contained in the basic scriptures.

Composed in technical language rather than in the everyday demotic of the *Sutras*, it subjects these themes to rigorous analysis – as well as the experiences generated by meditation on them – and turns them into the building-blocks of an integrated philosophical system. The most celebrated body of *Abhidharma* literature was written down, like the *Vinaya* and the *Sutras*, in the first century BC, in what is now Sri Lanka – becoming 'the Third Basket' of the so-called Pali canon. (Since then it has been much added to by later texts and commentaries.) This version, however, is the legacy of one particular sect. The *Abhidharma* of earlier sects – written originally in Sanskrit – survives both in fragments and, in two Chinese translations, in its entirety. The *Abhidharma* phenomenon, in fact, provides ample evidence of wide-ranging – and competitive – philosophical speculation.

The Monks and the Laity

It is likely that the *Abhidharma*, the *Vinaya* and some of the more recondite passages in the *Sutras* were reserved for the monks' exclusive use from the start. Some of the *Sutras*, indeed, suggest that the laity should not be burdened with anything too metaphysical or complex. What, then, was the exact relationship of the laity to the monks it was required to support, in the early period? And what were the monks' responsibilities towards the laity?

As well as being distinguished by the colour of their dress – monks wore red or ochre robes and householders white – lay-people and initiated members of the early *Sangha* differed, as we have seen, in the spiritual possibilities open to them. If a man chose to remain as a householder and family man, it was generally assumed that he had accumulated insufficient merit in his past lives to be able to shake off the day-to-day world and join the elect. His only present religious duty, therefore, was to go about the task again – to accumulate enough merit to be able to take a step up the spiritual hierarchy after his next rebirth. This he could achieve by a variety of means, some ethical and some practical.

First of all he had to commit himself publicly to the Three Jewels (Buddha, the *Dharma* and the *Sangha*), as we have seen – although he was allowed to retain his ancestral beliefs and any other Brahminic practices and rituals that were appropriate to his caste. (The Buddha makes no exclusive demands on his followers.) He also had to observe the Five Precepts: that is, to refrain (as far as possible) from killing living things and to eschew stealing, inappropriate sexual behaviour, lying and drinking alcohol. On regular feast days he could also commit himself to a further three of the Precepts: that is, to fast after the pre-noon meal, to turn his back on all worldly amusements (singing, dancing, dramatic performances, etc.) and to wear neither perfumes nor ornaments. More merit could be earned from sleeping on a low (rather than a high) bed and refusing to handle gold or silver – and yet more from giving up sex entirely and exchanging his white robe for that of a novice monk.

The most important responsibility of the layman, however, was to be generous – especially to monks. This involved regular donations of food and drink, as well as such items as robes, medicines and sandals – it also meant gifts of land and buildings. The amount of merit earned by each act of generosity depended in part on the spiritual status of the recipient and so *arhants* were especially favoured – as, of course, was the memory of the Buddha himself. Although many of the early structures that were donated or built by Buddhist laymen were made out of wood – and have hence disappeared – traces survive of dwellings that were cut out of rock or made from fired brick at around the beginning of the second century BC. During this early period, *stupas* and *stupa*-halls also appear to have been erected within monasteries to enshrine relics of the Buddha and locally revered *arhants*. Attendance at these *stupas* and *stupa*-halls – and at the many shrines which continued to dot the local countryside – involved several actions including ritual circumambulation (walking around), prostration and offerings of flowers. These actions fell short of what we today would call worship, but it too generated merit.

The cynical might say that this system of merit-gathering worked largely to the benefit of the monks, for they were then allowed to concentrate selfishly on their own salvation, without having to concern themselves with bodily survival. However, the monks – at first living isolated lives on the outskirts of villages or else deep in the jungle, and then only gradually gathering in monasteries from which they re-emerged each year to lead the mendicant life – provided a kind of glue that held the wider community together, both socially and spiritually. The monks were sustained without having to work, but in return they preached the *Dharma* and instructed the laity in morality, the afterlife and salvation through self-forgetfulness. They were also a living example of the freedom and serenity that the laity could finally achieve if they committed themselves to live ethically. Over time, a vast body of literature grew up that proclaimed the virtues of the secular life, including both cautionary tales (*avadana*) and so-called Birth stories (*Jakata*) that recounted the adventures of the Buddha in his previous lives, both animal and human. In these stories, constant stress was laid on rebirth, the lingering effects of *karma* and the virtue of treating all living things with respect.

There were, of course, and this was also stressed, personal

rewards to be had in return for faith and commitment. Both laymen and laywomen, that is to say, were sure to become 'stream-winners' at least and have only happy rebirths. The householder who lived in accordance with Buddha's teaching was also guaranteed increase of wealth, reputation and public standing in life and a death that had both direction and meaning. Women were offered the additional prospect of rebirth among the Gods of Lovely Form, as long as they were sweet-natured and amenable, respected their husband's relatives and guests, made their homes into pleasant and well-run places and protected their husband's valuables.

There was, however, a further benefit that the monks brought to the lay community – this was a collective one, fed by a widespread belief that economic prosperity and freedom from epidemics, hunger and war could only be guaranteed by adepts who understood and could propitiate unseen occult forces. This had been – and remained to a degree – the responsibility of the Brahmin priesthood, but it increasingly devolved on to the more humble and democratic shoulders of the so-called sons of Shakyamuni, with their ascetic way of life, their daily rounds and their stories. All was well with the people, it came to be assumed, as long as they respected the monks and gave generously both to them and to their foundations. This attitude became state policy, in effect, during the reign of King Asoka in the third century BC, for a nation had taken the place of the people by then.

Asoka

In about 320 BC, a nobleman called Chandragupta Maurya succeeded to the throne of Magadha and set about the business of conquest. Within two decades he had achieved suzerainty over huge swathes of the Indian subcontinent, from Bengal to eastern Afghanistan and as far south as the Narmada river. By the time his grandson Asoka inherited the Magadhan empire some thirty years or so later, it stretched far beyond central India to the country of the Tamils in the far south. Asoka only had to bring Kalinga (modern Orissa) in the north-east of India to heel to become master of virtually the whole subcontinent.

Asoka's campaign against Kalinga, according to legend, was swift, brutal and successful, but he was so horrified by the carnage inflicted by his men that he began to turn away from the world. It was then that he had a chance encounter with a Buddhist monk called Nigrodha, who persuaded him to use his enormous power to promote peace and virtue throughout his territories, instead of violence. Asoka soon took up the study of the *Dharma*, became a Buddhist layman and gave up the royal pursuit of hunting, since it broke the principle of *ahimsa*. He made pilgrimage, so the story goes, to Bodghaya, the site of the Buddha's enlightenment and built *stupas* – both at Kusinagra, where his body was cremated, and at Sarnath, where he gave his first sermon. Asoka also ordered the enlargement of a *stupa* dedicated to a former Buddha called Kanakamuni and provided, in an inscription, the first evidence we have of the doctrine and cult of other Buddhas who had preceded Siddhartha into the world.

According to tradition, Asoka built eighty-four thousand *stupas* in all as part of a hugely ambitious building programme that included wells, roads, hospitals, dispensaries and monasteries and that stretched all over his empire. He went on religious tours and held discussions with holy men, so it is said, of every sect. He also arranged for exhortations to be carved in every territory on rocks and pillars, recommending the ethical life to his subjects: these were his famous Rock Edicts, the first recorded writing in history composed by a Buddhist layperson:

> Do not perform sacrifices or do anything else that might hurt animals. . . . Be generous to your friends . . . Do not get involved in quarrels and arguments . . . Try to be pure of heart, humble and faithful . . . Do not think only of your good points; remember also your faults as well and try to put them right. . .

There is no mention of the inner arcana of the Buddhist faith in any of the Edicts (twenty-one of them issued in two groups separated by a gap of thirteen years), nor are the Four Holy Truths, the Eightfold Path, Nirvana or the supramondane qualities of a Buddha referred to. Indeed there is little or no reference to either meditation or the acquisition of wisdom. These omissions may well have been deliberate, since Asoka's aim was to build a bridge between the state and all of its people, drawing them together into one ethical community no matter what their faith or sect. (Or they might also have been due, of course, to the fact that the monks denied the inner workings of the Buddhist system to laymen, however high their worldly status.) To Asoka, *dharma* seems to have meant respect for all life (*ahimsa*), loving kindness (*maitri*) and the first four of the All-Is-Ists' perfections: giving, morality, patience and vigour. He lived by these principles and as the first Buddhist king he ruled through them – and so opened up another front for the faith: the achievement of the *Dharma* under political patronage and within the structures of government.

Asoka tried to communicate this message to other rulers through special *Dharma*-emissaries. One of his edicts records that he sent envoys to preach the *Dharma* to the post-Alexandrian kingdoms of Egypt, Syria, Macedonia, Epirus and Cyrene (in northern Africa) in

the middle of the third century BC. Although they had no traceable
effect there were better results closer to home, for an inscription in
Greek and Aramaic found in Kandahar, Afghanistan records Asoka's
efforts to 'make men more pious', and concludes:

> Acting in this way, during their present life and in their
> future existence, they will live better and more happily in
> all things.

Asoka's spreading of the Buddhist message may also have helped in
the later conversion of other monarchs of the post-Alexandrian age.
Kings such as the Indo-Greek king Menander (Pali: Milinda) in the
second century BC, whose debate with the monk Nagasena became,
as *The Questions of King Milinda* (*Milinda-Panha*), a small jewel in
the post-canonical literature; and the Scythian king Kaniska in northwest India, a century or so later. According to one tradition, it was
under King Kaniska's aegis, in Kashmir, that a final Buddhist council
on the subcontinent was held, to sort out once more the differences
within the *Sangha*. Legend has it that a monastery was built at the site
of the council and that five hundred monks sat down to engrave
agreed commentaries on the scriptures on copper sheets. These
sheets were then said to have been deposited in a specially-built
stupa – although no trace of it has ever been found.

It was in what is now Sri Lanka, however, that Asoka's legacy
most firmly took root. In about 240 BC, he despatched his son
Mahinda and his daughter Sanghamitta to the island as missionaries
and the result of their work is that Buddhism has flourished there
longer than anywhere else. It soon became the state religion. In the
words of Edward Conze in his authoritative *A Short History of
Buddhism*:

Only Buddhists had a legitimate right to be kings and the island of Lanka was held to belong to the Buddha Himself, It was the king's duty to protect the Order of monks and great benefits accrued to the monasteries in the form of donations, prestige and protection from interference. The kings, although mostly laymen, were also the final judges in any dispute which might arise among the Buddhists. The monks in their turn generally helped the kings and won popular support for their wishes. This close connection of the Sangha with the state had its disadvantages. From the second century BC onwards it not only infused a spirit of nationalism into the Buddhism of Ceylon and made the monks prone to political intrigue, but it also led them to enthusiastically support the national wars of their kings. They assured king Dutta Gamani (107–77 BC) that the killing of many thousands of enemies was of no account, because as unbelievers they were really no more than animals. They accompanied the army of the same king, 'since the sight of bhikkhus is both blessing and protection for us', and the king himself had a relic of the Buddha put into his spear.

Theravadins

Of all the eighteen different sects or 'schools' of Buddhist thought that tradition records in the early period, this one, the Ceylonese 'school' – known as the Theravadins – is the only one that has survived. Gradually, one must suppose, the entire canon of Buddhist literature found its way to the island. There, at a council near the village of Matale, in the first century BC, it was rehearsed, revised and finally written down on palm leaves, which were then consigned by the writers to the three baskets of the *Vinaya*, the *Sutra* and the *Abhidharma*. The canon was written in Pali, an everyday dialect of Sanskrit, and it is the most complete version of Buddhist scriptures that we know, since the canons of other 'schools' have mostly been lost. It is from later practices of the Theravadins (geographically isolated, for the most part, from later developments in Buddhism on the subcontinent) that we can infer some of the festivals that early Buddhists must have celebrated: the coming of the New Year (mid-March or -April), for example, and the Offering to the Ancestors (the beginning of October), both of which roughly coincide with the Hindu calendar. Most important of all, of course, was the joint festival of the Birth and the Enlightenment of the Buddha, both of which events fell by tradition on the full-moon night of the month of Vaisakha (April–May). It continues to be celebrated today.

Sacred Places and Worship

Early Buddhist art, archaeological findings and continuing Theravada practice also provide us with a reasonably clear picture of the way in which Buddhism incorporated pre-existing customs and lore in this period. It shared its view of the world and its picture of life as an ever-turning Wheel with Brahmanism, of course. Some of its elements reach back further still, to the tree-spirit and serpent-cults, the fertility goddesses and the reliquary mounds of the invaders who arrived in the Indus Valley from the central European steppes. In the myth of the Buddha, Queen Maya gave birth to Siddartha under a sacred tree and she is characteristically depicted as standing beneath it in the traditional pose of a fertility goddess. The Buddha himself, it should be remembered, died between two trees and reached Enlightenment beneath another, the Bodhi Tree (*pipal* or *ficus religiosus*), veneration of which is an assimilation (and takeover) of a very much earlier cult-practice.

The Bodhi Tree, in fact, seems to have fulfilled for Buddhists the role a sacred tree played all over India as 'the fulfiller of wishes' and the bringer of all desires, in every settlement in which it found itself. Garlands of flowers were hung on its branches and offerings placed on the altar at its base, which was usually surrounded by a fence of wood and stone. Asoka is said to have become so obsessed with the original Bodi Tree at Bodghaya that his queen tried to have it destroyed and it was he, by tradition, who turned it into a place of pilgrimage and a shrine. He placed a carved stone seat (the so-called 'diamond seat') in front of the tree which, though empty, symbolized the eternal presence of the Buddha.

As we have seen, *stupas* were also built by Asoka and others, both in cave-buildings and in the open, and these too were derived from earlier funerary practices: they had been traditionally built over the cremated remains of holy men and kings. Within Buddhism, they became the most venerated of all monuments, not only presiding over the ashes and relics of the Buddha and his *arhants*, but also commemorating miracles, laying claim to sacred spots and honouring the merit of their building in the name of the Buddha and the *Dharma*. The dome of a *stupa* is traditionally built over either a circular or square base and was – and is – called 'the egg' (*anda*). It represents rebirth, the potential transformation of the human spirit, and it not only commemorates the Buddha's death but also his entry into *nirvana*. (This, *mutatis mutandis*, was similar to the original symbolism – now mostly lost – of the Christian Easter egg.) At the pinnacle of the egg-dome rises a stone umbrella, the symbol of the Buddha's status 'as spiritual royalty', to use the phrase employed by Robinson and Johnson in their *The Buddhist Religion*.

In early Buddhist sculpture, we see Buddhists – and even serpents and gods – gathered round a *stupa* or a Bodhi Tree, their hands folded together in front of them in the traditonal way, some kneeling, some carrying garlands. Offerings, mostly of flowers (particularly lotuses), are laid out on shrines and altars, hung from branches or draped over a *stupa*'s dome. There are, during this period, no actual representations of the Buddha himself. Instead, he is symbolized by a variety of sculpted images: an empty throne; a pair of footprints; a wheel; a lotus; a shrine with a turban on it; and a circle beneath a tree. The empty throne, recalling the 'diamond seat' at Bodghaya, is a recollection of his Enlightenment and the footprints, often engraved with representations of the wheel and the Three Jewels – as well as swastikas (symbols of well-being in Sanskrit) – are a reminder that he walked the world among humans and left behind him a Path to be followed. The wheel is both the Wheel of Life and an aide-mémoire of his First Sermon at Srinath and the turban is a symbol of the wealth and power that he left behind him when he 'went forth'. The lotus, the most beautiful and the most ubiquitous of these images, has a symbolism all of its own. Growing out of the constantly shifting waters of becoming, it rises up out of the mire of existence and transcends it, just as the Buddha does.

Why no images of the Buddha were carved in, or have survived from, this early period remains a matter of speculation. Perhaps, in contrast to the vivid and teeming pantheon of Hinduism, symbols alone were thought sufficient to evoke his presence. Perhaps his Enlightenment was regarded as too ineffable for him to be represented in human form. Whatever the reason, the huge variety of images that we associate with Buddhism in the present day had to wait for the development of the movement which finally threw the esoteric knowledge of the monks open to the wider community of the Buddha's lay followers – Mahayana, the 'Great Vehicle or Course'.

Chapter Six:

Mahayana

The early period of Buddhism, as we have seen, was largely dominated by senior monks, who saw themselves as the sole caretakers of the Buddha's word – as indeed they were, in a literal sense, given that written texts did not yet exist in any organized form. They used their control over the oral transmission of the scriptures, however, to take on a further role, that of gate-keepers. They denied laypeople access to the Buddha's direct teachings, and downplayed the role of the laity in general and women in particular, whether ordained or not. Although Buddha had pronounced that salvation was available to any man or woman, whatever his or her status, the *Sangha* soon came to be divided into four categories – women, householders, nuns and monks – each (except for monks, of course) subservient to the category above. Even though lip-service was still paid to the Buddha's pronouncement that a householder was capable of becoming an *arhant*, there is little mention of this ever happening in the early literature. As for women, very few, even the most distinguished nuns, were thought worthy of mention after the first generation, although the first of their number had been Buddha's own foster-mother and aunt. A notable exception, of course, was

Saghamitta, who took a cutting of the sacred Bodhi Tree with her on her joint mission to Ceylon with her brother. But then she was an emperor's daughter.

Echoes of Dissent

Bubbling away under this increasingly rigid order of things, though, we can still hear the echoes of dissent. Among the eighteen 'schools', there were several which questioned – and sometimes denied – the privileged status of the *arhants*. (What goes up can still come down, they said.) Others questioned the monks' insistence on the futility and unreliability of individual consciousness and argued for a more commonsense view of the world. There was a feeling abroad, it could be said, that monks who cleaved narrowly to the received words of the historical Buddha – and interpreted them for their own benefit – were increasingly out of touch with real life and with the aspirations of lay people, who wanted equal standing and equal access to the spiritual rewards the monks so jealously guarded.

In the period around the first century BC this feeling, most clearly expressed in the early doctrines of the *Mahasanghikas*, first became a drift, then a movement and finally a wind that spread throughout the subcontinent and blew away the cobwebs and conservatism of the old establishment. It seems to have originated in two main areas – the south and the northwest – where local populations were most exposed to outside influences, both philosophical and artistic. In the northwest, for instance, Buddhists lived cheek by jowl with Brahmins and Zoroastrians; Indo-Aryans rubbed shoulders with Persians and Greeks; and some scholars believe that the *Mahayana*, the Great Vehicle or Course that Buddhism took around the time of the birth of Christ, owes much to the religions and iconography of the Iranian and Mediterranean worlds.

It also owes a great deal, of course, to a comparatively new and increasingly available technology: that of the written word. Central to the *Mahayana* is a literature, written in Sanskrit, that added to and embellished the scriptures of the Pali Canon – *and presented itself as equally authoritative*. The impulse behind this literature – which Edward Conze calls 'one of the most magnificent outbursts of creative energy known to human history' – is plain: it was designed to rejuvenate Buddhism, to prevent it from ossifying and to adapt it to a new age and new social conditions. It belongs very much to its time. Yet, for all this, it is made up of *Sutras* that, for the most part, purport to be absolutely authentic: the teachings of Buddha himself.

The Mahayanan Viewpoint

This was justified to some degree by the *Mahayana* interpretation of the essential nature of Buddha. Following the *Mahasanghikas*, Mahayanists belittled the significance of the Buddha's appearance in history: Sakyamuni the man, they maintained, had simply been the creature of a transcendental Buddha, who exists through all eternity and in all places as the supreme embodiment of the truth, preaching the *Dharma* at all times and in myriad forms. This clearly meant that he could also reveal new aspects of the Law – the new 'expanded' *Sutras* – wherever and whenever he chose. Furthermore, through his inspiration or charisma – on which Mahayanists laid great stress – he could infuse thoughts into the minds of his devotees and sustain their strength in the *Dharma*. Since he is eternal and omnipresent, it was plainly possible for his overpowering influence to pervade the minds of individuals to such a degree that their utterances – made however long after his disappearance from the world – would have the same value as his earthly teachings.

This was not, in fact, a defence that early Mahayanists ever articulated, for by then, in a sense, the die had been cast – they had already plumped for a mythological explanation. The new texts, they announced, had indeed been preached by Sakyamuni during his lifetime. However, at about the same time that the monks were codifying what later became the Pali Canon, at the first cave-council at Rajaghra, they had been collected and authorized instead by a council of *Bodhisattvas* (Buddhas-to-be) on the mythical mountain of Vimalasvabhava. Afterwards, they had been miraculously preserved by the Naga serpent-kings in their underwater palaces, ready for release when the time was ripe. 'Five hundred years after the Buddha's Nirvana', as the second-century AD sage Nagarjuna put it, 'when the good law, after having gradually declined, was in great danger', they were finally released into the world to give new life to the faith.

It is not altogether surprising – given this explanation of the derivation of the texts – that they should have been greeted with a good deal of scepticism by those who became known derisively by the Mahayanists as followers of *Hinayana*, 'the Inferior Vehicle or Course': even though *Hinayana* was to remain the most influential element within the Indian *Sangha* for another five or six hundred years. Being a Hinayanist, in fact, came to mean two things – rejecting the authenticity of the Mahayanist *Sutras* and continuing to cleave to the path of the *arhant*. Both came under increasing attack in the developing Mahayanist literature. At first, it has to be said, there was little disparagement. In *The Small Perfection of Wisdom*, one of the early 'expanded' *Sutras*, the description of the Mahayanists' innovative new spiritual hero, the *bodhisattva*, is put into the mouths of great *arhants*. A little later on, however, in another *Sutra*, *arhants* are described as being at a dead end, imprisoned in a nursery form of *nirvana*. Even the worst of sinners has a better chance of true salvation, says the *Sutra*. By the time of the *Lotus Sutra*, written in about AD 200, there is more or less open warfare. The *Lotus Sutra* describes those who do not believe the 'expanded *Sutras*' to be the words of the Buddha as wicked, and says witheringly of the *arhants* that since there is after all only one *nirvana*, even they might just be able to achieve it one day.

The many schools of *Hinayana* Buddhism have today more or less disappeared – their sole survivors are the Theravadins of Sri Lanka and their offshoots. So what is it about Mahayanist beliefs that made – and continues to make – them so attractive? Since Buddhism is first and foremost a doctrine of salvation, why did its particular path to salvation prove so popular and, given its successful export to almost the whole of eastern Asia, so universally applicable?

The Central Doctrines of *Mahayana*

Mahayanan beliefs can be separated out - as Edward Conze does - into five different categories.

1. The *bodhisattva*, driven by altruism and continually reborn into the world by choice, takes the place of the spiritually individualistic *arhant* as the pathfinder and exemplar.

2. A new road to salvation is mapped out in which compassion ranks as high as wisdom – and along which progress is made in the early stages via the six 'perfections'.

3. Faith – for initiate and layman alike – is given a fresh importance by

the creation of a new pantheon of divine beings, to whom worship, veneration and propitiatory offerings can be made.

4. A new virtue, 'skill-in-means', the ability to bring out the spiritual potential of others, is given priority in the attributes of a saint – even over wisdom.

5. A new coherent account of the nature of reality is given which, by advancing such notions as 'Emptiness' and 'Suchness', provides map-reference points to the whereabouts and nature of the Infinite.

The Bodhisattva *Ideal*

The *Bodhisattva* – or Buddha-to-be – was a familar figure to ordinary laymen through the *Jataka*, the elaborate folk-tales which recounted the adventures in previous lives of the Buddha on the way to his Buddhahood. The Mahayanists opened up this path to Enlightenment to the faithful, in effect, while downgrading the virtues of that taken by the *arhant* and the *pacceka buddha*. A *bodhisattva*, that is to say, is one who turns down the pursuit of salvation for himself alone and embraces instead the opportunity to return time and again to the world to help others. Anyone who aspires to this path first seeks to generate *Bodhicitta* or 'Wisdom-Heart'. This will ultimately allow him to preserve an Enlightened equanimity after rebirth amid the distractions and noise of the world of *samsara*, rather than pursuing Enlightenment through extinction and cessation, as the *arhant* and the *pacceka buddha* do.

Compassion and the Six Perfections

In the early period, it was the wisdom of the *arhants* – their complete understanding of life and of ultimate reality – that had been the paramount virtue. Wisdom, however, maintained the Mahayanists, could be, and was indeed being, turned to ends that were selfish. In fact, there was nothing in wisdom alone that required it to be used to help others. Only when it was combined with infinite compassion could the stain of selfishness – and, therefore, self-centredness – be avoided. As in the end the only truly unselfish entities were Buddhas – who were both all-wise and all-compassionate – theirs was the path to be followed in an unselfish quest for enlightenment. The way of the *bodhisattva* became known as 'the Buddha-Vehicle', a word that was more or less interchangeable with the word *Mahayana*.

Following it, however, was, and is, no easy task, for it requires a very precise balance – a marriage of equals, indeed – between wisdom and compassion. (It also requires countless lives and aeons of time.) Compassion – empathy with the suffering of the world and a desire to rescue all living things from it – is vital to the decision to keep on postponing entrance into the bliss of *nirvana* and to continue being reborn; and wisdom is essential to a deeper and deeper understanding, through successive lives, of the emptiness (*sanyata*) of all there is. Compassion is necessary if the *bodhisattva* is to identify with all living things and share their passions, as he must, even though wisdom reveals again and again that they, their passions and their travails are equally illusory and fictitious. Finally, the *bodhisattva*, who is only separated from Buddhahood in the end by his clinging and contaminating belief that he somehow remains a separate individual, has to learn to obliterate himself completely – and for this too both compassion and wisdom are required.

Compassion to enable the loss of self through sacrifice and service and wisdom to tear through the veils to ultimate reality and the 'own-ness' or 'is-ness' of all things.

According to Richard Robinson and Willard Johnson in their *The Buddhist Religion, A Historical Introduction*, the *bodhisattva* path begins

> with instruction from a Buddha, a bodhisattva or some other spiritual friend. Seeds of virtue are planted in the mind of the hearers, and from much hearing they come to perform good deeds, through which they acquire more and more roots of goodness. After many lives, thanks to the infused grace of the various teacher-saviours and the merit earned by responding to them, a person becomes able to to put forth the bodhicitta ('thought of enlightenment'). The two motives for this aspiration are one's own desire for bodhi and compassion for all living beings who suffer in samsara. Initially the motivation is both egotistic and altruistic, but along the path one realizes the sameness of self and others, and transcends the duality of purpose . . . 'Arousing the thought of enlightenment' is a decisive conversion experience with profound psychological effects. It is compared to a pearl, the ocean, sweet music, a shade-giving tree, a convenient bridge, soothing moonbeams, the sun's rays, a universal panacea, and an infallible elixir.

From this point of acceptance, through future aeons of time, the *bodhisattva* practises, and keeps to the path through the six perfections or *paramitas*, 'the methods by which we go to the Beyond'. Each involves a virtue – giving, morality, patience, vigour,

---

meditation and wisdom – which is practised to perfection when exercised without cost-counting, ulterior motives or self regard. Any merit earned in the process is reassigned to universal enlightenment and the spiritual welfare of other beings, rather than simply being held in a sort of individual bank account as a down-payment for future bliss.

The first perfection – giving (*dana*) – entails total and complete generosity of spirit, a willingness to give away every asset one has: material, intellectual, emotional, even life itself. The second perfection – morality (*sila*) – requires utter dedication to moral precepts, even in the face of worldly retribution and death. The third – patience (*ksanti*) – involves endurance in the face of hardship and avoidance of anger and forgiveness, but it also means meek acceptance of unpalatable, even at first sight incomprehensible, *Mahayana* doctrines such as that of the non-existence of all things, the fact that they neither arise nor cease.

Vigour (*virya*), the fourth perfection, represents the unflagging energy that the *bodhisattva* must perfect in order to pursue good works throughout the aeons and not be discouraged. Meditation (*dhyana*), the fifth perfection, is the ability to enter every kind of meditative trance and leave it again at will – without reaching towards whatever paradise it might offer. Wisdom (*prajna*), the last perfection, is the ability to understand the nature of all things and how they are related in the end: the unreality of their separate existence. It leads at its highest point, in the words of Conze, 'right into the Emptiness [*sunyata*] which is the highest reality'.

The doctrine of the six perfections, or *paramitas*, had first been promulgated by the heretical All-Is-Ists two or more centuries before, as we have seen. However, laity and monks alike were also familiar with it through the tales of the Buddha's previous lives in the

Jataka. Born as a hare, for example – and having decided to practise the perfection of giving – the Bodhisattva was approached one day by the god Indra, disguised as a brahmin, who asked him for food. Having no alternative he offered himself, telling the brahmin to light a fire and cook him. In another life, he demonstrated his vigour by ceaselessly trying to find water when his caravan had run dry in the desert; and in yet another life, reborn as a mariner, he achieved great feats of navigation through wisdom, despite the fact that he had gone blind. Reborn into a further life as an ascetic, he ran foul of a ruler, who demanded to know what doctrine he now espoused. 'Patience', he said. After the ruler had instructed his executioner to flog the Bodhisattva, he asked again and got the same reply. Finally, the ruler had his hands and feet cut off, followed by his nose and ears, but the Bodhisattva still professed his patience and, so the story goes, felt no anger.

Folk-tales like this were moral lessons – they encouraged their listeners to follow the example of the Bodhisattva. After hearing such stories, the hearer perhaps felt that it was not too great a step to become a Bodhisattva himself: to follow his path.

The New Pantheon

Having achieved the six perfections – and having come face to face with the reality of Emptiness – the Mahayanist *bodhisattva* could now, if he chose, leave the world of suffering and enter *nirvana*. If he did this, though, it would mean the end of his mission, so he elects to remain in order to go through the last four of what came to be known in Mahayanist doctrine as the Ten Stages. At this point, however, although he is still in the world he no longer belongs to it. He has instead become a supernatural being with miraculous powers and 'sovereignty over the earth' – a 'celestial Bodhisattva' – and as such, of course, worthy of worship and veneration. The faithful soon turned to a host of Bodhisattvas – twenty-three of them are mentioned in the *Lotus Sutra* – of whom a number are worth examining further:

Maitreya: Maitreya is the object of the earliest *bodhisattva* cult of all. He is first mentioned in a Pali *Sutra* as a Buddha-to-be who will finally arrive in the world and command an even greater following than Sakyamuni. Acknowledged by all Hinayana sects – and still regarded by Theravadins as the only true *bodhisattva* of the present age – he is both a living compassionate presence and, in his present birth, a god. He can thus be worshipped by Buddhists and theists alike.

Manjusri: Manjusri ('gentle or sweet glory'), another Bodhisattva at the tenth stage of his journey to Buddahood, is the personification of wisdom and eloquence. By performing certain actions, such as worshipping him, meditating on his representations and teachings and chanting – or even hearing – his name, various benefits accrue to his followers: from happy rebirths and guarantees of future enlightenment to an appearance of the Bodhisattva himself. He takes on the form of a poor man or orphan and appears before his devotees either in the real world or, if their sight is obstructed by bad *karma*, in their dreams.

Avalokitesvara: Avalokitesvara (probably 'the lord who looks down') is described in a third century *Sutra* as an omnipresent, omnipotent saviour-deity who can take on any guise – Buddha, *bodhisattva* or god – to help living things save themselves from the snares and perils of *samsara*. He also guards his devotees against lust, anger and folly.

Usually represented as a bejewelled layman wearing a high crown and often carrying a lotus, he became revered in Tibet as the country's patron-protector, worshipped through his mantra, *'Om mani-padme hom'*. Later, in China, he took on the form of a woman and is now worshipped as a Madonna-like figure throughout east Asia, under a variety of names that echo his original Chinese ideogram, *Kuan-Yin*, or 'sound-regarder'.

Samantabhadra: Samantabhadra, in a late passage of the *Lotus Sutra*, is described as arriving in the world with an elaborate retinue to ask Sakyamuni to expound the *Sutra*, of which he became, in effect, the protector and guardian. He wards off human enemies and demons from the monks who keep the *Sutra*. Mounted on a white elephant with six tusks, he is present to jog their memory should they forget any of the words during its recitation. He will also provide inspiration in person and give talismanic spells to any devotee who follows a rigorous programme of worship by circumambulation.

Celestial Buddhas

In addition to Celestial Bodhisattvas, the Mahayanist pantheon also admitted a new class of Celestial Buddhas that derived, at least in part, from early and accepted teachings. It will be remembered that Sakyamuni discouraged his disciples from venerating him as a person, on the grounds that this kind of adoration was misdirected. 'Whoever sees me, sees the *Dharma*. Whoever sees the *Dharma*, sees me' he was reported to have said – that is, 'concentrate on the *Dharma*'. He also said, in the version of the *Diamond Sutra* quoted by Edward Conze:

Those who by my form did see me,

And those who followed me by voice,
Wrong the efforts they engaged in,
Me those people will not see!

From this arose the view that the Buddha in fact had two bodies: a physical body and a *Dharma*-body. His physical body, for all his wishes, became an object of veneration after his Enlightenment – it was given the thirty-two major marks of the superman and was reputed to give off rays in six colours, as well as a heady perfume. The 'real' Buddha, however, was thought to lie in his *Dharma*-body. By the time the *Mahasanghikas* pronounced that the Buddha was eternally active, both transcendent and immanent, in the world – and that he had created his physical body merely as a convenience – it seemed reasonable to assume that these 'conveniences' existed, like the *Dharma*, in all places and in all realms. In fact, there had to be Buddhas both in the past and in the future – and in every possible corner of existence. In a remarkable prefiguration of modern theories of alternative universes, early Mahayanans posited up to a billion different worlds: in at least a proportion of those worlds, a *Tathagata* – or 'one who has come or gone to the True', as Sakyamuni preferred to call himself – lives, teaches and embodies the *Dharma*.

These myriad 'Buddha-lands', as they were known, lay in all possible directions, and in many ways they were similar to the heavens of the gods, except that they remained, however delightful, a staging-post on the way to the ultimate goal of *nirvana* (which every inhabitant was ultimately guaranteed). They were not in any sense final resting-places (like the paradises, say, of Christianity and Islam), nor were all their denizens confined to them, for both Buddhas and *bodhisattvas* could appear at will anywhere else in any of the other worlds where living beings needed their help. Supernatural intervention, that is to say, was available to the faithful who asked for it.

Aksobhya: Aksobhya ('imperturbable') is the earliest mentioned of the Celestial Buddhas, inhabiting a Buddha-world to the East. He can be thought of as the patron and sponsor of angerlessness in his devotees. He is usually represented as blue, with a blue elephant, holding a pure diamond in his right hand and making the 'earth-witness' gesture with his left.

Amithaba: The origin of Amithaba ('infinite light') probably owes a good deal to Iranian sun worship. He has a Buddha-world in the West called Sukhavati ('happiness-having') – a land of eternal daylight suffused with the colours of the rainbow, where his devotees (later known in China as the Pure Land Sect) are offered an existence full of ease and pleasure. Even the worst sinner, if repentant, can still gain access as long as he has faith. In the seventh century, Chinese travellers recorded that Amithaba had many worshippers in India – he later became a major cult figure in the Far East, where he is known as Amito (China) and Amita (Japan). In literature he is often conflated (or confused) with another Celestial Buddha, Amitayus ('unlimited-lifespan'), who is almost certainly derived from the Iranian Zurvan Akaranak ('Unlimited Time'). Both Celestial Buddhas probably originated in the borderlands between India and Iran, where Buddhism had a strong presence (see below).

Vairocana: Vairocana ('shining out') came to be regarded as the *Dharma*-body of Sakyamuni. (The word was orginally an epithet applied to him.) Sun and light imagery played a major part in early accounts of Sakyamuni and his Enlightenment. His knowledge was light shone into the darkness of ignorance, he revealed himself with a light-shaft beaming from the eye of wisdom on his forehead and his

Enlightenment coincided with daybreak. Vairocana only became popular as a Celestial Buddha in the seventh century, which was comparatively late, but he played a central role in the form of Buddhism that was to enter Japan two hundred years later. He was known in Japan as Dainichi, or 'Great Sun' and was seen as the 'Cosmic Buddha' who pervaded the entire universe. When Jesuit missionaries entered Japan in the sixteenth century, they used the word 'Dainichi' as a translation for their word 'God'.

'Skill-in-Means'

'Skill-in-means' (*upaya*) is the quality that a *bodisattva* acquires at the seventh stage of his path towards Buddahood after he has achieved perfection of wisdom. That is, when he fully understands the fact that nothing really exists except Emptiness, that the whole edifice of Buddhism – the Buddhas, the Bodhisattvas, the perfections, the stages – is a fiction designed to assist living things towards the one Ultimate Truth, which alone can liberate but about which nothing can be said which is not false and fleeting. Compassion alone under these circumstances would ordinarily be mute – wisdom alone would see the futility of all communication, but 'skill-in-means' supervenes over them and attempts to find the best way of bringing out the spiritual potential in others by appropriate statements and actions. The aspiring *bodhisattva* accepts that absolute truth is beyond thought and description, but also recognizes that there is such a thing as commonsense everyday truth which, although distorted, can still be manipulated to point the way. Ordinary language, for all its faults, is still a recourse for the *bodhisattva*, because the salvation of all things in the end depends on it.

The Nature of Reality

Mahayanan ontology is derived from that of the Mahasanghikans and it constitutes – as Conze says – the inner core of Mahayanan doctrine. The teachings, however, are complex, recondite and hard to summarize, partly because the nature of ultimate reality is unavailable to intellectual enquiry and remains beyond the reach of words, as is recognized in the texts themselves. All the teachings can do, therefore, is to point somewhere in the right direction – they cannot, in the nature of things, explain anything or say anything definitive. They are, to this extent, a series of signposts to a place that can never be found in this life, map-references to the whereabouts of the unknowable.

Early Buddhism had decreed that the *dharmas* – the psychological-cum- experiential particles which make up both the world and our perception of it – are characterized by impermanence, suffering and absence of self (no-self or *anatman*). Mahayanists, following the lead of the Mahasanghikans, delved deeper into this sub-atomic theory of reality and consciousness, as it were, and added a fourth characteristic: that of Emptiness. All *dharmas*, they said, were empty (*sunya*) and therefore basically indistinguishable from one another. They were both non-existent and one and the same.

This wasn't a particularly radical departure on the face of it, since Buddhist theory had always accepted the essential emptiness of the concept of self. This time around, however, it was a matter of emphasis. For by emphasizing and stressing Emptiness, Mahayanists were at the same time downplaying the central importance of the impermanence and suffering to which the world was systematically doomed – and from which monks had been encouraged to retreat. If all things were empty, after all, then aversion to the day to day world was empty too – and was no solution. If everything, indeed, was marked by an identical Emptiness, there was no relevant difference between the relative and the absolute, between *nirvana* and *samsara*, or between the *Buddhas* and *Bodhisattvas* and the men and women they guided. 'Own-beings' of any kind – with some sort of inherent, enduring and self-sustaining essence – simply did not exist anywhere at all. Intellectually they were fictions and emotionally they were the focus of obsessions and passions that enslaved and achieved nothing.

The Mahayanan concept of Emptiness further reduced any perceived imbalance that remained between the (spiritually privileged) monks and the laity. Also, because it implied emptiness of thoughts, it provided a new object of contemplation – that is, Emptiness itself – as a form of therapy that was effective both intellectually and emotionally. This did not imply or involve turning one's back on the world, in any sense, or denying that things in it have existence. On the contrary, it meant confronting the world and its sense-objects in their Suchness (*tathata*), 'such as they really are', without adding to them or subtracting anything from them at all. Suchness and Emptiness are, to the Mahayanan, interchangeable concepts and understanding this fully is the foundation of True Knowledge, in which all seeming oppositions – between subject and object, perceiver and perceived, affirmation and negation – are obliterated once and for all.

Beyond this point, of course, there was – according to Mahayanist doctrine – well, nothing: just Beyondness, the enveloping silence of the ineffable and unknowable. The nature of the path to it – depending as it did on the same-egg-twin concepts of Emptiness and Suchness – was to have a profound effect on religious life, however, as Robinson and Johnson point out in their *The Buddhist Religion: A Historical Introduction*:

Monks in training who are ridden with feelings of guilt and shame because they have infringed the Vinaya are told to appease their guilt by meditation on its emptiness. This does not give them license to sin, but it liberates them from the burden of evil. The bodhisattva can work and play in the secular world without fear of contamination from sense objects, because he knows that intrinsically they are neither pure nor impure. He associates with merchants, kings, harlots, and drunkards without falling into avarice, arrogance, lust, or dissipation. He accepts and excels in the arts and sciences, welcoming them as good means to benefit and edify living beings. He recognizes the religious capacities of women, listening respectfully when they preach the Dharma, because he knows that maleness and femaleness are both empty.

Even in their abstruse ontology, then, the Mahayanists acted as a democratizing force within the *Sangha*, one that served gradually to erase the old embedded divisions. They also showed considerable elasticity, as we have seen, in their absorption of elements from the beliefs of other peoples and religions. These two characteristics of Buddhism's new broom, taken together, not only explain why it became the dominant school in India itself in the end, but also, perhaps, why it was supremely successful as an export.

Early Mahayanan Sects

During what might be called the middle period in the development of *Mahayana* doctrine – that is, in or about the second century AD – there appears to have been a huge change in Indian culture, a change that could perhaps be summed up as The Rise of the Individual. Not only was there a new confidence in ordinary people's ability to arrive at knowledge without the intercession of gods or saints, but there was also an effloresence of secular literature, poetry, fiction and social and historical observation. There were advances in science, new developments in logic, raised standards of debate and, above all, named authors. From then on, named initiates of the Mahayanist school – virtually all of them monks, it seems – began to produce treatises that relied increasingly on personal experience and rational argument. They still routinely invoked the *Sutras* as evidence, of course –and *Sutras* continued to be written to provide new evidence and proofs wherever necessary – but the practice of Buddhism from then on had a human direction and face. What Konze calls 'the unsystematic phase' in the building of *Mahayana* doctrine began to come to an end.

Nagarjuna

One of the first great *Mahayana* sages whom we know by name as a historical personage is Nagarjuna, a southern Indian philosopher of genius who, at the end of the second century AD, founded what came to be known as the Madhyamikha school, or 'the school of the Middle Way'. Nagarjuna had very little to say about trance, meditation and altered states of consciousness. Instead he brought a ferocious intellect to his exposition of Mahayanist doctrine, through which he more or less bludgeoned into submission non-Mahayanist assumptions about the nature of reality.

Nagarjuna – whose most famous work is the polemical *Middle Stanzas* (*Madhyamaka-karikas*) – is, in a sense, the Indian Socrates. Firstly, like Socrates, he professed no views of his own – instead, he used his opponents' arguments to demonstrate that their implications flew in the face of the very assumptions they were based on. Secondly, he ruthlessly used the tool of the dialectic to demolish pairs of opposites that were routinely used to describe reality: unity and diversity, permanence and annihilation, coming and going, etc. By demonstrating how these opposites ended up negating each other, he produced what has been called a theory of universal relativity – one that prefigured Einstein's – by showing the conflicting effects of points of view (the man on the moon, the man who points to it, the man on the spaceship rushing by, etc.). He deconstructed the world of perceived reality, announced that all statements about it were ultimately untenable and pointed the way to where ultimate truth had to be positioned – that is, in the middle (hence 'The Middle Way'), in a place without point of view or angle of vision, where the urgent interior cinema of thinking and identifying had been switched off.

Yogacarans

Another school that can be identified with known historical figures is known as *Yogacara* ('Yoga Practice') or *Vijnanavada* ('Teaching of Consciousness'), which flourished in northwest India in the fourth century AD, under the aegis of two brothers, Asanga and Vasubandhu. These adepts chose a different pathway towards the unknowable than that taken by Nagarjana and his followers: it was based on psychological rather than intellectual theory. In other words, they attempted to answer some fundamental questions about the mind and the way in which it constructs the illusory world: questions at the heart of Buddhist doctrine, which remained unresolved. If, for example, what we perceive as the world is a fleeting and impermanent mind-construct, by what processes exactly do we create and objectify it from moment to moment? If sense-impressions are as ephemeral as their objects, which of them actually apprehends each object and how exactly does the world – or rather our construction of it – present itself as continuous even though it is forever dying away? What exactly is memory? How does it work? Above all, perhaps, what is the 'it' that experiences absolute truth, when 'it' is finally free from the mind-constructed shackles of illusion?

They started from the position that everything, even the Absolute, can be described as Mind, Thought or Consciousness – hence the name of their central doctrine, *citta-matta* ('mind only' or 'nothing but consciousness'). To explain how this central principle 'created' the world, they posited the existence of a 'store' or 'foundation' consciousness, a version of Jung's 'collective unconscious' in which the seeds of potential phenomena are stored and from which they constantly pour out to be made manifest in perception. They equated this 'store consciousness' with what they called *tathagatagarbha*, or 'the womb of Enlightened Being-ness'. However, *Garbha* – the 'womb' part of the word – means not only the womb but also the womb's contents: the embryo or developing child. For them, 'store consciousness' was not only the place where the Enlightened Being was conceived and matured, but it was also the embryonic Buddha himself who inhabits the 'store consciousness' of each individual.

In essence, this theory stems from an earlier doctrine – that the effects of good and bad *karma* are transmitted between lives as seeds, which ripen and bear fruit later, at their appropriate time. In the writings of the Yogacarans, however, this concept was expanded to include not only the embryonic presence of Buddha (the divine) within each one of us but also the stock of good *dharmas* generated by the universal power of his radiance. If these were not present in consciousness, they argued, how could there exist any impulse towards the religious life? Why would anyone choose to reject *samsara* and take up the difficult road towards *nirvana*? No, the womb/embryo was present in every living being – pure in its nature and synonymous with Suchness. In ordinary and ignorant people, of course, it was smeared and sullied over by the contaminants of *samsara* – impurities even remained in *bodhisattvas*. Only in Buddhas was *tathagatagarbha* pure and unsullied, right through to its core.

The storage of good *dharmas* and Eternal Being-ness in consciousness is the Yogacarans' contribution to what we might today call the psychology of conscience or the impulse to good. However, the Yogacarans' concept of *tathagatagarbha* also had intensely practical consequences. Since it was 'store-consciousness' which was responsible for what was in effect a hallucinatory illness – the projection of the twin delusions of the world and our 'independent' psycho-physical engagement with it – a cure was clearly available. The cure lay in learning to penetrate beyond these yoked chimeras by way of trance and meditation, so that one could finally arrive at a state of pure consciousness that was stripped of content and beyond the fake 'I-it' duality of appearances. The path to this lay in and through what the Yogacarans called 'the three natures': the absolute; the relative; and the imaginary. The imaginary – mistaking a coiled rope for a snake, for example – had first to be cleansed little by little through meditation, like a series of stains, from the relative. Things in the world had to be seen and confronted as they really were, with nothing added or subtracted. At this point, the relative (the world seen for what it actually is) could be gradually pared away too, until nothing remained of it and 'an act of cognition which no longer apprehends an object' could be achieved. This state, pure consciousness, with neither thinker nor thought, was the ultimate goal of Yogacaran trance-medicine and was where salvation lay.

The *Yogacara* (or *Vijnanavada*) school produced another refinement in Buddhist thinking, one related, in a sense, to its notion of 'the three natures' (the Madhyamikhans recognized only two). This was its doctrine of the Three Bodies of Buddha, a doctrine which was to achieve some importance later. It had earlier been proposed, of course, that the Buddha must have had two bodies – his 'apparition' or 'form' body, the *ad hoc* phantom sent by the real Buddha to do his work on earth and the *Dharma*-body or Absolute Truth: the *Mahayana*-proposed embodiment of *nirvana*. To these two bodies the Yogacarans added a third: the 'recompense' or 'enjoyment' body. This is the body, acquired in reward for his career as a *bodhisattva*, in which the Buddha shows himself to *bodhisattvas* and other superhumans when he preaches the *Dharma* to them in other realms. The Buddha Amitabha, for example, spreading joy and delight in his kingdom of Sukhavati, is portrayed as appearing to the *bodhhisattvas* in his 'enjoyment' body, while at the same time making his presence known to his devotees on earth in the 'apparition' version of himself.

The Spread of Mahayanism

We have already seen how King Asoka sent his own son and daughter as Buddhist missionaries to the island of Lanka. Tradition has it that more of his emissaries arrived in what is now Thailand to establish the religion there among its original inhabitants, the Mon people. Another early success story for Buddhism is likely to have been Nepal, for after all Buddha himself was born there, at Lumbini, and King Asoka is said to have visited his birthplace to erect an inscribed pillar.

(Another of his daughters is said to have married Nepal's king.) Although almost nothing is known of Nepal's early history, a legendary version of events has it that the Bodhisattva Manjusri came to Nepal from China, emptied the great lake which had filled the valley, founded the capital of Kathmandu and then installed as ruler King Dharmikhara, whom he had brought with him.

However, the most important area in the history of the development of Buddhism lay in the northwest of India, away from Nepal and the northeast, with its associations with Buddha, in a great sprawl of territory that today includes parts of Kashmir and the Punjab, Pakistan, Afghanistan, Iran and what was until recently Soviet Turkestan. At its heart was the province or district of Gandhara, centred around Purishupara (modern Peshawar), the first town of any size to greet the traveller making his way towards India after crossing the Khyber Pass. The whole area around Peshawar was one of the world's great crossroads and meeting places and early Buddhists – many of them the All-Is-Ists (*Sarvastivadins*), who had been voted down at the Council in about 250 BC and had migrated here – were exposed to influences from all over Asia and the Graeco-Roman world.

Important trade routes passed through the territory and so did conquering armies, as well as successive waves of nomadic tribes, from the time of the Aryans onwards. The army of Alexander the Great arrived in the fourth century BC, routing local Persian dynasts before finally downing arms in the Punjab, desperate for home. Some of Alexander's soldiers and generals, stayed on, however, and they were soon joined by other peoples: Scythians, Parthians, Kushans and Huns in search of pasturage, conquest or trade. It is not surprising that this northwestern entrepot of peoples and cultures became one of the main breeding-grounds of the supple, assimilative creed of

Mahayana, as well as the main springboard for Buddhism's remarkable journeys to the north and east.

None of this, of course, happened overnight. In fact the religion does not seem to have taken real root in the northwest until the time of King Asoka, who had lived as a Viceroy in the area as a young man. (He is said to have founded five hundred monasteries for the *arhants* and to have given the valley of Kashmir to the *Sangha*.) A century or so later, the religion was given another shot in the arm by the conversion of the Greek king Menander (or Milinda), whose power base lay in Bactria, a fertile region in northern Afganistan between the Oxus river and the mountains of the Hindu Kush. (His conversations with the monk Nagasena are recorded in the Pali text, the *Milinda-panha*). The Indo-Greek hegemony, though, did not last long, for it was soon supplanted by yet more invaders, this time Scythians and Parthians. It was not until another empire, that of the Kushans, began to take shape that Buddhist influence once again started to predominate.

The Kushans were a nomadic people who had originated in China. They had travelled a roundabout route – through central Asia to the Kabul valley in northern Afghanistan and then southwards into the low country of India, consolidating their rule along the way. The empire they established in the process stretched across the whole of northern India, eastward to Sinkiang (Chinese Turkestan) and westwards almost as far as the Aral Sea. Although they were at first hostile to Buddhism, the Kushans became both believers and enthusiastic builders of monasteries and *stupas* in the end, particularly under another convert, their first century AD king Kaniska. In fact, Kashmir, with its many *Sarvastivadins*, became an extremely important centre of Buddhist learning from Kaniska's time onwards. Most major Buddhist scholars whom we know by name seem to have spent some time there – from Asvagosa, the first century AD Sanskrit poet who wrote the first biography of Buddha, to Asanga, the chief philosopher of the Yogicaran school. In an essay produced in the late 1950s, 'Some Great Buddhists After Asoka', Bharat Sing Upadhyaya wrote (as quoted in John Snelling's *The Buddhist Handbook*):

> Kaniska's reign . . . marked a turning point in the history of Buddhism and Buddhist literature. It witnessed the rise of Mahayana Buddhism and the magnificent literary activity started by Parsva, Asvagosa, Vasumitra, and others . . . It was in this age that Pali gave place to Sanskrit [as the literary and liturgical language of Mahayana]. In the field of art, Gandhara sculptures developed and the figures of the Buddha and Bodhisattvas began to appear. It was during Kaniska's reign and largely through his efforts that Buddhism was successfully introduced into central and eastern Asia. There was ceaseless literary activity throughout his vast empire . . . A truly integrated Asian culture came into existence at this time, based as it was on the highest purposes of life for which Buddhism stood.

Even though the Kushan dynasty was later overthrown by the Sassanids, who were Zoroastrians from what is now Iran – and Buddhism lost its royal patronage – the religion continued to thrive in the territories of what had been the Kushan heartland. Some time between the third and fifth centuries BC, for example, the famous cave-monasteries at Bamiyan in northern Afghanistan were dug out and the standing Buddha that was carved there became the world's largest stone statue at 177 feet high – although it was recently destroyed by the Taliban. Kashmir – although it went through many ups and downs as ruler followed ruler – was to remain an important Buddhist stronghold for a further thousand years after the time of Kaniska.

Not so the area immediately around Peshawar, however, where Buddhism fell victim to the depradations of yet more invaders, the so-called White Huns – and to a gradual revival of Hinduism, encouraged by the princelings who had taken over the remnants of the Kushan empire. When the famous Chinese traveller Hsuan-sang passed through Peshawar in the seventh century AD, he found it to be a dismal and mostly uninhabited place. Almost all of the monasteries were ruined and deserted.

Buddhism in Central Asia: The Silk Road

By then, however, Buddhism had already moved on into Central Asia, carried along the trading routes of the great Silk Road which ran between China and the West. Today, this vast oblong of desert and mountains is deeply inhospitable but two thousand years ago, before the glaciers dried up, the climate was wetter. There was irrigation and agriculture and there were important oasis-settlements that were virtually small city-states, some of them dating from as early as the third century BC: Turfan, Kucha and Kashgar on the northern spur of the Road and Khotan on the southern spur,. Having started life, no doubt, as caravan halts, they were consolidated under the Chinese Han dynasty (206 BC – AD 220) and were soon home to an astonishing variety of peoples who spoke languages related to Sanskrit, Latin, Greek, Persian and even Celtic.

Some of these so-called Serindians, judging by the evidence of surviving frescoes, were fair-haired with blue or green eyes. Included in their number were Manichaeans, fire-worshippers and Nestorian

Christians: one fresco found in Turfan (modern Kao-chiang) seems to show a Palm Sunday procession. Within the last century, archaeologists have discovered that their languages were written down in a modified Indian script whereas their art was essentially Gandharan, with Graeco-Roman, Sassanid and Chinese influences. However, their literary and sacral language was Sanskrit and their chief religion was Buddhism.

What little we know of the Serindian (or Sino-Indian) culture, apart from the archaeological record, comes to us from Chinese foreign-policy documents and the written accounts of later Chinese travellers. The picture that emerges is of industrious, sophisticated and independent kingdoms, kept in balance by Chinese watchfulness and trade. (One of the kingdoms was almost certainly the 'people in the west' to whom the Han Emperor Wu sent an expedition in 139 BC to 'make an alliance'.) They produced silk, jade, taffeta, felt and woollen goods and the musicians and artists of Khotan were famous. During the period of the first known travellers, sometime around the third century AD, Khotan was home to five thousand Buddhist monks and acolytes who lived in a hundred different monasteries. Meditating *arhants* also lived in mountain-caves to the south, where their hair was cut regularly as a religious duty by monks from the city. Before it finally died away, Khotan was to become an important centre for *Mahayana* Buddhism, but the first accounts from eye-witnesses, dating from the third century, suggest that there was a balance of some sort between Hinayanans and Mahayanans. We know this because when a Chinese pilgrim arrived in about AD 260, looking for a more or less complete text of the *Perfection of Wisdom Sutras*, he was warned by Hinayanans not to take back with him a *Mahayana* manuscript that might corrupt the Chinese people!

Whatever the original balance of the two sects, though, in this and the other oasis-states, it was the teachings of the *Mahayana* that achieved dominance in Central Asia. This was almost certainly because Mahayanists were a great deal more flexible than their opponents in their interpretation of the scriptures. Hinayanists continued to live under the rigorous monastic discipline of the *Vinaya* (as they did in Kucha), which forbade the practice of medicine. They were also bound to withold the *Dharma* from the nomadic peoples of Central Asia, who characteristically drove herds and ate meat. Cleaving stolidly to the core of Buddha's teachings, they also failed to adapt themselves to local beliefs and practices – which, from what little we know, seem to have been enthusiastically embraced by local Mahayanists. For example, the monks in Tun-huang appear to have practised both medicine and Central Asian shamanism, judging from the accounts we have. They had a reputation for magic powers as well as clairvoyance and clairaudience.

Tun-huang (now known as Dunhuang), which lay at the Chinese end of the Silk Road before its bifurcation into two branches, may also provide another reason for the ultimate dominance of *Mahayana* as virtually the only form of Buddhism that was to take lasting root outside India – for it was also a translation centre. In the third century AD, under the leadership of Dharmaraksa, the so-called '*bodhisatta* of Tun-huang', many of the central documents of *Mahayana* were translated into Chinese (and perhaps other languages) including the *White Lotus of the True Dharma Sutra* and the *Perfection of Wisdom*. Another translation centre was established later on in Kucha, under a saintly sage called Kumajariva. Once again it was preoccupied with Mahayanist texts like the *Diamond Sutra* and the lay-directed *Vimalakirti-nirdesa*, the story of a rich householder whose compassion was so great that he chose to take, even as a layman, the path of the *bodhisattva*. It was said that monks were afraid to visit Vimalakirti, since he could always beat them in argument.

The sheer scale of this essentially Mayanist enterprise was not uncovered until almost a thousand years after every last trace of Buddhism and its art had been brutally erased by Muslim conquerors and after the faith had fallen back into the desert. In 1888, a British officer called Hamilton Bower bought an ancient Sanskrit medical text written in Brahmi characters while on a secret mission to Kucha. When news of this and other discoveries leaked out, virtually all the imperial powers sent archaeological expeditions to the area as quickly as they could. They not only found texts and manuscripts in a huge variety of languages but also statues and frescoes, which they hacked down from walls and packed off to the world's museums. The greatest discovery of all, though, fell to the British Sir Aurel Stein, for in Tun-huang he found over a thousand temples and shrine rooms carved into a cliff, a vast Buddhist monastic complex. He also found an astonishing cache of paintings on silk and, above all, a huge collection of manuscripts in a cave that had been sealed off in about the year 1000. There were texts in long lost languages, historical and financial documents, vernacular Chinese versions of Buddhist writings – and the oldest printed book in the world, published in AD 868: a Chinese translation of the *Diamond Sutra*.

China

In the first century AD – so the story goes – the Chinese Han Emperor Ming Ti dreamed of a giant man sixteen feet tall, sending out great waves of light. He despatched emissaries to the west in search of him and somewhere on their journey they met two *bodhisattvas* in the desert, who had with them a white horse, a picture of the Sakyamuni

Buddha and a copy of the *Sutra in Forty-Two Sections*, a still-extant summary of Buddhist doctrine infused with Mahayanist thought. They were invited by the emissaries to return with them to the Han capital of Loyang, where they began translating the *Sutra* into Chinese at what became known as the White Horse Temple, a site that still exists. It is a charming story, but the reality is almost certainly a lot more prosaic. Buddhism entered China gradually through the constant comings and goings of the great Silk Road. Buddhists from Central Asia – musicians and artists from Khotan, artisans and merchants – travelled eastwards (as well as westwards) by stages, before finally taking up residence in the Han capital and a few other northern cities. There they formed small emigré communities which must sooner or later have welcomed and supported monks travelling east with the Silk Road's caravans. These saffron-robed figures cannot have had much early success with the indigenous population as proselytisers of the faith – what, after all, could any barbarian possibly teach a citizen of the 'country of the sublime at the world's centre'? Nonetheless, with time, the monks must ultimately have lost their curiosity value and have become a more or less familiar urban presence. The monks' predilection for magic might even have made the Chinese regard them as being closely related to their own shamans and wizards.

However the idea, for all this, that this small seedbed of monks and nuns would one day grow into a vast Chinese *Sangha* would have struck them as being frankly ludicrous. For not only were the Chinese notoriously xenophobic but they also practised a worldly ideology that was profoundly unsympathetic to the idea of individual liberation. This was Confucianism – derived from the sayings of Confucius, the sage from the sixth century BC – which proclaimed the ideal of a harmonious social order in which everyone, from the highest to the lowest, knew his or her place exactly. Within Confucianism, correct ritual was everything and every aspect of life was mediated by strict codes of behaviour. To deny the importance of these things, to be indifferent to both family and country, to be prepared to cut off all worldly ties in pursuit of some vaguely-defined spiritual objective – as Buddhists were — was clearly the most shocking of heresies. Such behaviour served to undermine the bonds which held the Chinese state together under the Son of Heaven.

Taoism

There was, however, another Chinese tradition, one which resonated with the influx of Buddhist ideas: the tradition of Taoism. This was popularly believed to have been derived from the sayings of the Yellow Emperor, Huang Ti, who is said to have ruled from 2698–2597 BC, but it had been fully formulated and given shape by the sage Lao Tzu in his classic work, the *Tao Te Ching*. Taoists, unlike Confucianists, were hostile to the social world and its values, which they saw as dishonest and meaningless. Convention and slavish obedience, they taught, should be abandoned for simplicity and one-ness with the cosmos.

Their ideal was *wu-wei* ('non-doing' or 'non-action'), a totally spontaneous form of behaviour – unpremeditated and undirected, unconcerned with doing good deliberately – which we might translate as 'going with the flow' of the *Tao* (the 'Path' or 'Cosmic Way'). Being in harmony with the *Tao* meant being able to respond without forethought, when action was called for, to any and all circumstances in an appropriate way, since it both drew from and furthered the impersonality and supra-mondanity of the mode of the *Tao* in action and at work – *wu-wei*. There was within Taoism, moreover, a strong mystical and meditative tradition. One-ness with the *Tao* – which was Absolute and yet empty, according to Taoist philosopher Chuang Tzu – could be achieved through contemplative exercises.

It is not surprising, then – given this coincidence of doctrines – that the first translations of Buddhist texts into Chinese drew strongly on the ideas and vocabulary of Taoism. The Sanskrit word *marga* (or 'Path'), for example, was readily translated as *tao*, 'the way to be travelled'. Emptiness became *pen-wu* – the 'Original Non-Existence' of Lao Tzu; the 'Void Filled to the Brim' – which like a womb carries all existence within it. Even the Buddha became identified with the Taoists' 'Spirit in the Centre of Existence', or World Soul. Sometimes, early Buddhist treatises carried direct quotations from the *Tao Te Ching*, such as: 'The Holy Man's good works are mighty as Heaven and Earth, yet he is not humane' – thus equating the *bodhisattva*'s detached compassion with the workings of the *Tao*, which is indifferent to the individuals who pass along it. They even sometimes abandoned Buddhist orthodoxy in their anxiety to strike a chord with Taoists, as in this quotation, again from the *Tao Te Ching*: 'The body suffers destruction, but the soul undergoes no change. With its unchangingness it rides upon changes and thus passes through endless transformations.' Until the fifth century AD or so, many Chinese, indeed, seem to have considered Buddhism as simply another method of achieving the *Tao*. An early Chinese pamphlet even refers to Buddhism as being born out of 'the conversion of the Barbarians by Lao Tze'.

This Taoist form of Buddhism was widely spread abroad by the Mahayanist texts that were first chosen for translation into Chinese: notably *The Small Perfection of Wisdom Sutra* and the *Vimalakirti-nirdesa*, the story of the formidable layman who followed the *bodhisattva*-path. (The *Sukhavati-vyuha*, the account of the Celestial

Buddha Amithaba and Sukhavati, his Buddha-kingdom in the West, was also translated in the second century AD, though it was some three hundred years before his cult – Amito in Chinese – took hold.) The *Perfection of Wisdom* literature, with its teachings on the nature of perfect wisdom and emptiness, in fact proved especially popular – more and more of its *Sutras* were soon translated and so were technical handbooks on Buddhist-style meditation.

Central Asian Buddhism, in the gradual process of its sinification, not only acquired its first vocabulary from Taoism but also something of its suaveness and irreverence. (At an early stage, Buddhist monks became known in China for their urbanity and wit.) Furthermore, in tandem with Taoism, it benefited a good deal from the collapse of the Han empire (AD 220), and from the so-called Period of Disunity (220–589) that followed. With the coming of war and chaos – during which China was divided, first into three and then into two (northern and southern) kingdoms – the imperial social glue of Confucianism lost its adhesiveness. The aristocratic and artistic élite began to look elsewhere, that is to say, for their spiritual needs and the Buddhist message about a suffering and impermanence that can ultimately be escaped from was well suited, one can imagine, to the tenor of the times.

Buddhism also held out the prospect of a personal salvation, it should be remembered, which was an idea new to the Chinese. It had acquired shamanistic elements in Central Asia and its meditational techniques offered the possibility of acquiring supranormal powers. Its teachings, at the same time, were sophisticated and complex, which must have appealed to the Chinese literati, and it invited withdrawal from the world for the purposes of contemplation – a refuge devoutly to be wished in times of strife. In this period there appears for the first time what was to become a

Chinese-Buddhist archetype: the gentleman-scholar devotee surrounded only by nature.

Buddhism also had considerable appeal to two other important levels of Chinese society: the ruling classes and the ordinary peasants. The emperors of the various kingdoms – even of the northern one, the domain of the Mongolian invaders of the Northern Wei dynasty – saw Buddhism as either a way of positively undermining Confucianism (the northern view) or of keeping the population tractable and unwarlike (the southern view): or both. Buddhist monks were a lot more amenable, after all, than their Taoist equivalents, who were inclined to rebel against convention. Unlike the Taoists, who financed their own places of worship, Buddhists relied on donations from wealthy laymen and were thus less inclined to upset the *status quo*. Buddhists, above all, though, with their views about the killing of any living thing, were eminently peaceful – and peace, in a country often at war but without universal conscription, was highly desirable.

As to the masses, they were perhaps drawn first and foremost to the doctrine of the *bodhisattva*-path, which provided equal access to the most esoteric mysteries – even to the lowest of the low. (The *Vimalakirti-nirdesa* was, for this reason, one of Buddhism's most important recruiting tools.) In the enlarged Buddhist pantheon – in Celestial Bodhisattvas like Maitreya and Avalokitesvara and Celestial Buddhas like Amithaba and Aksobhya – they found objects of worship who offered encouragement, comfort and help in trouble. Furthermore, by supporting the *Sangha* they were assured of yet more benefits in future lives. It was generally believed in China that supporting the *Sangha* would greatly impress and influence the decisions of Yama, the God of the Underworld.

For all of these reasons, Buddhism soon ceased to be a fringe religion in China and became, in effect, the main stream. By the middle of the third century, a Chinese version of the *Vinaya* (monastic code) had been produced. A hundred years later, Chinese Buddhists were given official permission (in the eastern kingdom of the Chin rulers, at least) to enter monastic communities. In the south, Buddhist monks became important court advisers and counsellors and they received imperial patronage, even in the northern 'barbarian' kingdom of the Wei dynasty. Huge numbers of monasteries, temples, pagodas and *stupas* were built there and when a northern army finally conquered Chin and entered its capital at the beginning of the fifth century AD, its commander ordered his troops to protect and preserve all *Sangha* property, to erect Buddha images and to provide homes for all monks.

This was important, because the Chin capital, Chang-an, had become by then the most important centre for the translation of Buddhist texts in the whole of China and it was to become the birthplace of the first native Buddhist philosophers. The reason for this was that the great Central Asian sage and translator Kumarajiva had arrived there in about 401, after being carried off from Kucha by a Chinese general seventeen years before. He had been quickly appointed Director of Religious Instruction and a translation bureau had been set up for him, with, it was said, eight hundred assistants. With their help – and in what Arthur Waley describes as 'an infinitely agreeable' style – Kumarajiva set about translating or retranslating more than a hundred works, including the *Diamond Sutra* and the first versions of four important *Madhyamika* documents, which introduced the teachings of Nagarjuna to the Chinese.

Two of Kumarajiva's disciples were of equal importance in the ultimate development of Chinese Buddhism. The first of these was Seng-chao, who was said to have literally 'held the brush' for his master, since he had earlier been a copyist of Confucian and Taoist texts. Seng-chao, however, also produced a work of his own, *The Book of Chao (Chao Lun)*, in which he attempted to convey the Buddhist notion of emptiness through Chinese and Tao-derived versions of the oppositions that Nagarjuna had demolished in order to point the way. His book, rooted firmly in the Chinese language and concepts, represents the first thought-through indigenous Buddhist philosophical system that we know.

Another (younger) disciple of Kumarajiva was Tao Sheng, who seems to have been eminently practical for in one of his treatises he wrote (as quoted by Conze):

> Ever since the transmission of the scriptures eastward, their translators have encountered repeated obstacles, and many have been blocked by holding too narrowly to the text, with the result that few have been able to see the complete meaning. Let them forget the fish-trap and catch the fish. Then one may begin to talk with them about the Way.

Tao Sheng's practical nature might well have encouraged him to propose, in a treatise of his own, what was at the time an essentially new doctrine, that 'Buddhahood is achieved through instantaneous enlightenment'. He argued that since the absolute emptiness of Nirvana was totally different from all conditioned things, then the moment of Enlightenment also had to be quite different from everything that might have preceded it. All else was mere learning, confined as it was to the phenomenal world. Enlightenment, by contrast – being 'genuine' and 'permanent' rather than 'temporary' and therefore 'false' – could only be achieved all at once, in its totality, and not in any gradual, bit by bit way, 'for when the single enlightenment comes, all the myriad impediments are equally brought to an end'. Later in the fifth century AD, an official wrote of this doctrine, in witness to its practicality (again quoted by Conze):

> The people of China have a facility for comprehending Truth intuitively or 'mirroring' it, but difficulty in acquiring learning. Therefore they close themselves to the idea of accumulating learning, but open themselves to that of one final ultimate. The Hindus, on the other hand, have a facility for acquiring learning, but difficulty in comprehending Truth intuitively. Therefore they close themselves to the idea of instantaneous comprehension, but open themselves to that of gradual enlightenment.

Practical or not, though, Tao Sheng's doctrine later became of central importance in the development of Chinese, and later Japanese, Buddhism. It became the foundation of the so-called Chang school in China and found its expression in Japan (as we shall see) as Zen. It also marked the coming of age of Chinese Buddhism as an independently developing religion.

A number of sects or 'clans', it is true, continued to adhere to the philosophies of the Indian schools. *San-lun* derived from The Three Treatises school (*Madhyamika*) and Fa-hsiang owed its philosophy to The *Dharma*-Mark school (*Yogacara*) – the most famous member of which was the so-called Great Traveller, Hsuan-tsang, who made a sixteen-year pilgrimage to India, mostly on foot, and brought back with him over 600 Sanskrit manuscripts. But Chinese Buddhists were increasingly concerned with the adaptation of the Buddhist Canon to fit their own needs, language and forms of worship. In about 402, for example, an ex-Taoist called Hui Yuan helped to found what later became known as the Fellowship of the

White Lotus, which was dedicated to the worship of Amidhaba (Amito) and to rebirth in his Buddha-kingdom in the West. This was the nucleus of the later Pure-Land (*Ching-tu*) school, which continued to rely on the benign intercession of Amidhaba as the one way of reaching Nirvana. Amidhaba and the other Celestial Buddhas, together with all the Celestial Bodhisattvas with the exception of Maitreya were, it should be remembered, the creations and gifts of *Mahayana*.

Chapter Seven:

Tantra:
The Third Turning of the Wheel

Indian Origins

When the Chinese pilgrim Hsuan-tsang arrived in India in about AD 640, he recorded that only about forty per cent of the monks he encountered there belonged to the *Mahayana*. The rest, one must assume, were Hinayanists of one school or another, who were dedicated in their writings to commentaries and endless systematizations of their *Abhidharma* literature – and given more to piety than to either missionary work or spiritual innovation. Although, as another Chinese traveller later put it, the sects 'rest in their own places, and do not get themselves embroiled with one another', it is remarkable that in all the Hinayanist literature there is hardly a mention of the *Mahayana* at all. It is as if, for Hinayanists, Mahayanans had passed beyond the horizon of things that needed attending to – as if, with their 'extended' *Sutras* and their teeming celestial pantheon, they had gone beyond the pale of traditional orthodoxy into another realm entirely.

In a sense, of course, they had, and Hinayanists had been left behind by them simply to mark time, doing what they had always done – which was to keep the rules of the *Vinaya* and to consolidate the legacy of Sakyamuni as laid down in the *Sutras* and the *Abhidharma*. Over the years they had produced a vast literature out of these scriptures, covering every theme and detail that could possibly be dug up from them. They meticulously recorded the views of different teachers and to the popular Buddha-tales of the *Jataka* they added their own long accounts of the Buddha's virtues and his adventures in previous lives. (They also produced, in the *Buddhacarita* of the poet and playwright Asvaghosa, the first 'biography' of the Buddha ever written.) But by the beginning of the fifth century AD, their job was finished, The well of creativity had finally run dry – it was as though there was no more to be said. Vasubandhu, one of the last great commentarists and synthesizers of *Hinayana*, seemed somehow to sense this, for he finished his exhaustive work, the *Abhidharmakosa*, with the words:

> The times are come
> When flooded by the rising tide of ignorance
> Buddha's religion seems to breathe its last.

It did not breathe its last, of course. Although *Hinayana* produced little more original literature it continued in India for another 800 years and flourished for much longer in Ceylon, Burma and Thailand, as we shall see. However, a new wind had already begun to blow through *Mahayana* Buddhism, roused in the frontier lands of the northwest and the northeast and fed by both Brahminism and local occult practices. It was the last great contribution of the subcontinent's turbulent spiritual climate to Buddhist thought and it became known as *Tantra*.

Tantra

Tantra, like yoga and *bhakti* ('religious devotion'), is not in any sense exclusive to Buddhism. It is a recognizable part of the *ur*-spring of the Indian religious impulse surfacing, in various forms, in Jainism as well as Hinduism. Its adoption into the mainstream of Buddhist thought, therefore, should be considered as yet another opening-up of the faith to accommodate all of the subcontinent's peoples and religions into one mighty flow. It set out to achieve this, it could be said, by borrowing wholesale from them all, but then it too had been born out of the same spiritual aquifer. Sakyamuni had long before permitted his followers other forms of worship; and besides, the magic practices which Buddhism now incorporated remained pointing towards the ultimate goal of Enlightenment.

Edward Conze recognizes three phases in the development of Tantra:

> The first may be called Mantrayana [the 'Secret Mantra Vehicle' or 'Mantra Path']. It began in the fourth century, gained momentum after AD 500, and what it did was to enrich Buddhism by the appurtenances of magical tradition. In this way many mantras, mudras [ritual gestures of the hands], mandalas [ritual versions of magic-circle diagrams] and new deities were more or less unsystematically introduced into Buddhism. This was, after 750, followed by a systematization called the Vajrayana [the 'Diamond Vehicle' or 'Diamond Path'], which coordinated all previous teachings with a group of five Tathagatas ['Enlightened Beings']. In the course of time, further trends and systems made their appearance. Noteworthy among these is the Sabajayana, which, like the Chinese Chan school, stressed

meditational practices and the cultivation of intuition, taught by riddles, paradoxes and concrete images, and avoided the fate of turning into a dead scholasticism by holding on to no rigidly defined tenets. [Finally,] in the tenth century, we have the Kalachakra, 'Wheel of Time', which is marked by the extent of its syncretism and by its emphasis on astrology.

Conze's first phase, *Mantrayana*, almost certainly had its roots in early Buddhism, for magic had been specifically allowed into the Pali Canon in the form of spells (*parittas*) against such dangers as snake-bite. From there it was but a short step – taken by *Mahayana Sutras* as early as 200 BC – to the introduction of spells in the form of repeatable verbal formulae that were said to represent the doctrine of the *Sutras* (*dharani*) and to the borrowing of auspicious and powerful magical syllables such as *Om* from Hinduism. Over time, a vast phantasmagoria of gods, spirits, daemons, ogres and terrifying spirits, drawn from indigenous cults, was added to this base – probably inspired, to a degree, by the visions of Yogicarans in their advanced meditative states. From Brahmanism came esoteric yoga practice, including *Hatha Yoga*, along with popular magical rituals, instructions for ceremonials, mantras and perhaps even sacifices.

The most important of Buddhism's borrowings from the great spiritual pool of popular Indian religion, though, was that of the guru, prefigured in the *Bhagavad Gita*'s account of Krishna as the divine preceptor from whom knowledge of all mysteries comes. The new spiritual hero of this phase in Buddhist development, that is to say, was no longer the *bodhisattva* but the *siddha* – the 'magician', 'adept', or 'wonder-worker' – whose role it was to show his disciples (*chelas*) the Way. Although the ultimate goal still remained Buddhahood or

Enlightenment, it was no longer a goal that had to be put off for aeons and aeons – it could be achieved here ('in this very body') and now ('in the course of one single thought') under the instructions, and through the example of, the *siddha*-guru. With his help, all that had to be done was to transform the body and its attributes into those of a buddha, by means of special – and often secret – practices that involved processes and powers beyond the range of normal awareness.

One result of this new relationship between the *chela* and the *saddhu* was an inevitable decline in the authority of the monastic system, for individual *saddhus*, with their bands of submissive disciples, could easily dismiss as unnecessary the constraints of collective discipline. (Some of them, indeed, made mock of conventionally cloistered monks with wantonly heretical behaviour and teachings.)

Another result was the appearance of a wholly new kind of literature – Tantric handbooks (*Tantras*) – secret documents designed, not for the many, as the *Sutras* and *Sastras* ('treatises') had been, but only for a chosen initiated few. These not only covered meditational practices but they also included rituals which often (deliberately) flew in the face of standard Buddhist precepts and were given a new importance as sacraments. A vast majority of the *Tantras*, then, were written in so-called 'twilight speech', an ambiguous and mysterious form of language which clearly relied on individual interpretation by an adept. Substitution codes figure widely in 'twilight speech': semen, for example, is known as 'camphor', '*bhodhicitta*' or 'elixir'; male and female genitalia are 'thunderbolt' and 'lotus'; and sexual union is 'compassion'.

This disguising of secret practices almost certainly stems from the Yogacarans, whose founder Asanga, in one of his treatises, classified the various methods by which a hidden meaning could be conveyed. Opacity, imprecision and coding alike were seen by him as necessary, not only to keep out the uninitiated, the careless dabbler, but also to protect the teachings from contamination.

The erotic element in Tantra – of so much interest to the West – is perhaps best summed up by a remark in the *Hejavra Tantra*:

> Those who have 'means' are liberated from the bondage of
> 'becoming' through the very thing by which wicked people
> are bound. The world is bound by lust, and released by the
> same lust.

Before we explore this theme further, however, it may be useful to look at the background of Tantric symbolism and ritual against which it should be placed. Tibet, where *Tantra* was preserved in a relatively pure form until modern times, is the main source for our knowledge of these practices, although they have also survived in the so-called Shingon school in Japan.

The Tantric Pantheon

In some ways, *Tantra* can be seen as a response to adversity and the steady erosion of passing time: a renascence of Hinduism; a loss of direction; a slackening of support for the *Sangha*; or drift. The path of the *bodhisattva* – like that of the *arhant* earlier – had become overshadowed by the popular worship of the Celestial Bodhisattvas and Buddhas. The faith needed new protection from the inroads of the world and at the same time it also needed a new immediacy, a way of commanding attention among ordinary people, in order to turn them once more to Enlightenment.

Both protection and immediacy were provided by the magic of

a fresh pantheon of deities (*yidam*), both male and female, a pantheon which –although often borrowed from elsewhere – coincided with the supernatural beings encountered by the Yogacarans in trance. (From the doctrine of Emptiness, which held that there was no essential difference between *nirvana* and *samsara*, it followed that these trance-visions were no less real and actual than anything else in the world.) Some of them, like Tara and Avalokiteshvara, were seen as welcoming and beatific, and were represented as holding their hands up in benediction to the faithful. Others, although equally beneficent in their way, like the *vidyaraja* ('kings of the sacred lore' also known as 'protectors of the *Dharma*'), were presented as terrifying, 'wrathful', fierce fighters against Buddhism's enemies. This was also the role of the so-called 'Five Protectresses' – with Mahamayuri, the 'Great Pea-Hen', at their head. They were all pictured in much the same way – as snarling, fanged, enflamed avengers, often carrying skulls, daggers and severed heads.

With time, the pantheon increased to include further objects of cult worship that had evolved from, and were turned towards the needs of, three separate Buddhist groups. Those who practised advanced meditation turned to Cunda, Vasudhara and other goddesses; others, who pursued magical powers, looked towards the 'Queens of the Sacred Lore' and the *dakinis*, or 'sky-walkers'; and the masses were encouraged to worship particular goddesses to meet their different needs, such as guarantees of motherhood, immunity from smallpox or the protection from spiritual and physical danger provided by Tara (an early Celestial Bodhisattva). Later still – based on the model of the Hindu god Shiva, often depicted as having sex with his consort or *Shakti* – Buddhas and Bodhisattvas were given consorts of their own, (*Vidyas* and *Prajnas*) whose cult became one focus of erotic Tantrism.

Mantra

Mantras, as we have seen, are magical formulae, generally Sanskrit, the purpose of which was to protect the initiate against malign forces. In Tantric Buddhism, however, they also serve two other important and inseparable functions. The first function of a mantra is to evoke a deity, so that the initiate can become one with him or her, and the second function is to act as an object of meditation in itself, thereby enabling the initiate to gain insight or mental calm through repetition (although a mantra can also be visualized or written down). The most famous of all mantras, of course, is '*Om mani-padme hum*' ('*Om* in the lotus a jewel, hail!'), but there are many other celebrated examples, a number of them invoking and expressing oneness with particular goddesses. '*Om tare tuttare ture svaha*', for instance, although it is now not easily translatable, is a play on the name of the goddess Tara and '*Gate, gate, paragate, parasamgate, bodhi svaha*' ('Gone, gone, gone beyond, utterly gone beyond, enlightenment hail') enshrines and summons the goddess of Perfected Wisdom *(Prajna-paramita)* who, like Tara, was earlier worshipped as a Celestial Bodhisattva.

Other mantras, sometimes in short form, sometimes in long, affirm the truth of the doctrine of Emptiness: '*Om sunyata-jnana-vajra-svabhavatmako ham*' ('Om I am a self whose essence is the diamond knowledge of emptiness') – or the emptiness of both the self and the dharmas: '*Om svabhavasuddhah sarva-dharmah svabhavasuddho ham*' ('Om by essential nature all the dharmas are pure; by essential nature I am pure'). To their number should be added what are called Bija ('Seed') mantras, a vowel or consonant which embodies the essence of a particular Tantric deity. It can be visualized as a luminous form, from which the deity emerges.

Mandala

The mandala is a highly evolved version of the magic circle that has been familiar since prehistoric times as the marker-off of a sacred spot from the profanity of its surroundings. It is based – in part at least – on the form and architecture of early *stupas* which, with their railings separating sacred from profane ground, were also designed as material maps or enshrinements of the Buddhist cosmos. When representations of the Buddha became general in the first century AD, Buddha-images were characteristically placed at certain key points of the symbolic design of both the *stupa* and the courtyard surrounding it. The *stupa* was thus transformed, in a sense, into a three-dimensional version of the mandala – while the mandala represented in two dimensions the cosmology embodied in the *stupa*.

The mandala, then, is first of all a visual mnemonic of the way in which the Buddhist scheme of things revolves around the central hub of Mount Meru. It is also a model of the individual human being, in whom the drama of the universe is reproduced in microcosm around the heart-centre, where the mystery of ultimate reality (known as *Mahamudra*, 'the Great Seal') is located. More than that, with its four gaps or doors on its periphery, it is a representation of the spiritual journey each initiate undertakes once he or she has chosen to enter the Path – travelling through the concentric precincts of deities and demons in their labyrinthine. towered palaces towards the focal sanctum where the Supreme Being which guides him or her holds sway.

The particular genius of *Tantra* was, and is, that it transformed the creation of mandalas into a process that Robinson and Johnson call 'actualization'. A mandala, that is to say, was no longer merely regarded as a representation of the cosmic and human setting of the quest for enlightenment. It became the very arena in which that quest was conducted, a ritual space in which communication with gods and other worlds was made possible. With the help of the diagram in meditation, the initiate could become the Buddha at the centre of the mandala, could confront primordial fears and passions in the shape of demons and could summon up gods by the use of the syllable of the *Bija* mantra that constituted their occult principles. By this means, latent spiritual potentials buried deep in the psyche of the practitioner could be unlocked, and he could learn to travel in the Buddhic universe, far beyond the reach of *samsara*, dominating and dissolving its gravitational pull at will. This was, of course, a potentially dangerous enterprise, as is stressed again and again in traditional Tantric texts. Dabbling without proper instruction from a *siddha* could cause a burn-out like that of Icarus, who travelled ill-equipped and too near the sun. For this reason, the making of mandalas and the actualization of divinities are governed by strict rules and precisely-defined rituals in *Tantra*, as a protection again the psychic damage that could be carried forward into future lives.

Ritual Objects and Gestures in Tantra

Mudra, literally 'a seal' or 'symbol', is a traditional ritual gesture of the hands carrying a symbolic – both communicative and interiorized – meaning. In *Tantra*, different *mudras* relate to different aspects of a particular Tantric deity.

Tibetan *Tantra* also makes use of ritual objects – particularly the *ghanta*, or bell, which symbolizes the female principle of wisdom, and the *vajra* (literally 'the lord of stones'), a single or double sceptre derived from the thunderbolt wielded by the Hindu god Indra. The *vajra* represents 'skill-in-means' and the diamond-like quality –

uncuttable by any other substance but itself – of the *nirvana* or ultimate Emptiness that can only be arrived at through the marriage of 'skill-in-means' to (the bell of) wisdom. Other important objects in Tibetan ritual are the dagger (*phurba*), the skull-cap (symbolizing impermanence) and the thigh-bone trumpet.

The *Vajrayana*

Around AD 750, as we have seen, the myriad spiritual and magical elements which had been assimilated into Tantric Buddhism from Hinduism, from aboriginal and animist cults and from the esoteric doctrines of the Yogacaran school of *Mahayana*, were systematized by the *Vajrayana* (the 'Diamond Vehicle' or 'Path'). From this time on, all cosmic forces were grouped into five classes, each of them presided over by a *Tathagata* ('Enlightened Being' or *Dhyani-Buddha*) of their own. The Five classes comprised Vairocana, Aksobhya, Ratnasambhava, Amitabha and Amoghasiddhi, and between them they represented the five primary energies responsible for all creation. They were linked together by a dense web of interpenetrative symbolism, by an endless series of 'magical correspondences', as Conze puts it, of 'identifications, transformations and transfigurations', bringing together 'all the forces and facts of the universe'. He goes on:

> The body in particular is regarded as a microcosm, which embodies the entire universe and is the medium for realizing the truth, very largely by methods which form a part of what is nowadays known as Hathayoga in India. We hear much about parallelisms between the visible, the audible and the touchable, and everything is designed to unite the powers of mind, speech and body for the purpose of realizing the final state of completeness, or

enlightenment. The Vajrayana has been well defined as 'the art of living which enables us to utilize each activity of body, speech and mind as an aid on the Path to Liberation', and in this way it is astonishingly akin to the contemporary Chan school [in China]. The true meaning of Vajrayana teachings is, however, not always easy to ascertain, because here it has become a convention to clothe the highest into the form of the lowest, to make the most sacred appear as the most ordinary, the most transcendent as the most earthly, and the sanest knowledge is disguised by the most grotesque paradoxes. This is a deliberate shock therapy directed against the over-intellectualization of Buddhism at that time. The abundant sexual imagery in particular was intended to shock monkish prudery. Enlightenment, the result of a combination of wisdom and skill in means, is represented by the union of female and male in the ecstasy of love. Their becoming one in enlightenment is the highest indescribable happiness (mahasukha).

The erotic element in *Tantra* teaching was not, of course, merely shock treatment for prudish monks, a sort of all-out attack by heavy metaphor for, in the consorts given to Buddhas and Bodhisattvas the sexual symbolism of bell and sceptre, etc. the union of male and female in *Tantra* was central. Part of the early revolution in Mahayanist thinking had been the promotion of a marriage between wisdom and 'skill-in-means' as a necessary step towards enlightenment. Wisdom was soon conceived as a goddess, and *Tantra* raised 'skill-in-means' to the same status. It is from the union of these two divine beings in *Tantra* – physical as well as symbolic – that *bodhicitta* ('Wisdom-Heart'or thought of enlightenment) derives.

Tantra, that is to say, fuses spiritual with physical love in certain of its rituals, both in idea and in practice. In Tantric texts, the relationship with one's deity is compared to the four stages of a relationship between a man and a woman (looking, smiling, touching, having sex) and *bodhicitta* is seen as finally arising from the explosion of orgasm. Robinson and Johnson give an example of how the spiritual and the physical are related in this:

> In the mandala of Hejavra, the goddess Nairatmya ('No-self') stands for Wisdom, and Hejavra stands for means. When the mandala is acted out, the yogin impersonates Hejavra, and his consort takes the part of Nairatmya . . . The rites are practiced long and thoroughly in contemplation before they are actually performed. The yogin imagines the mandala and the goddess around the circle and mentally envisages the rites with himself as the deity. Having conjured up this vivid drama, he contemplates that these phenomena, like all others, are empty – that there is neither subject nor object, thought nor thinker . . .

... and then he plays his part

One tradition maintains that this sort of sexual ritual is only to be practised under certain very special and controlled circumstances – and then only by advanced practitioners who have already generated *bodhicitta*. Other texts deny this – erotic rites are recommended elsewhere for those who are driven by hostility and must cultivate compassion and loving kindness. It seems most likely in the end that eroticism in *Tantra* is simply a part of its general thrust (so to speak), which is to sacramentalize every sort of human activity and yoke it to the pursuit of enlightenment. No activity is to be forbidden, because all activities, of whatever kind, whether forbidden by Buddhist precept or not, are equally empty. This belief had been prefigured by Vimalakirti, the famous layman *bodhisattva*, in the *Sutra* that recounted his life. Many of his sayings, quoted by Robinson and Johnson, have a distinctly Tantric feel:

> Only for conceited men does the Buddha preach that separation from lewdness, anger and folly is liberation. For men without conceit, the Buddha preaches that lewdness, anger and folly are indeed liberation . . .

> The bodhisattva seems to proceed in precept-breaking, yet persists in pure morality. He seems to proceed in the passions, yet is always pure in mind. He seems to have wives and concubines, yet always keeps far away from the mud of the five lusts . . .

> Just as lotus flowers do not grow on a high plain of dry land but only where there is low, moist mire, even so, only in the mire of passions are there living beings to produce the Buddha-qualities.

The *Hejavra Tantra*, of a much later date, explains, in a sense, this paradox, when it says:

> The unknowing worldling who drinks strong poison is overpowered; he who has expelled delusion, with his mind on the truth, has dispelled it utterly. . . The expert in poison repels poison by that very poison, a little bit of which kills most people.

Tantra: *The Third Turning of the Wheel*

Use the passions, in other words, to kill the passions. As in Rabelais'
Abbey of Thelema, do what you will shall be the whole of the law.
Nothing is forbidden to a true seeker. What may be dangerous or tabu
to ordinary people is available to an initiate – so long as he enters it
under the guidance of his guru and within the sacred precincts of the
mandala. If he crosses the boundaries of Buddhic precepts, it has to be
done with a pure mind – and not for personal pleasure.

The second reason to believe that erotic magic lay somewhere
close to the original heart of *Tantra* is that there were considerable
efforts made to cleanse it of its physical elements at an early date. By
around AD 800, that is to say, *Tantra* had become, in effect, an
academic subject. At the great Buddhist university at Nalanda, and at
other new centres set up in eastern India by the Pala kings of Bengal,
scholars were writing commentaries, providing keys to 'twilight
language' and explaining the symbolic meaning of objects and actions
– making *Tantra*, in other words, respectable. If everything was mind,
they argued, then mental exercise alone could perfectly reasonably
take the place of any physical engagement.

As a result, many Tantric sects, it is said, gave up their attempts
to sacralize, indulge in tabu behaviour and explore the farther reaches
of human experience and instead turned to pure contemplation.
(Some of them did not, and there are many references to various illicit
practices in Tantric texts, including incest, drinking, cannibalism and
eating the flesh of cows, elephants, horses and dogs.) For all this,
though, in Tantric teaching the human body remained, and remains, a
supremely important arena for the drama of the struggle for
enlightenment. The male and female body, in the Tantric physiology,
has four pyschic centres – the navel, the heart, the throat and the brain
– which are connected by various channels (*nadi*) along which there
are a number of special plexus points, or *chakras*. A so-called wind-

173

energy – which can be interpreted as consciousness – circulates through this system, but in ordinary people, whose channels are knotted and blocked, it manifests itself in unregenerate passions like greed, rage and desire. It is the responsibility of the follower of the Path – using the tools of mandala and meditation (and perhaps also sex) – to gradually unblock the channels in order to allow the wind-energy free circulation. Once that has been done, he can, by psychic means, attempt to direct and dissolve the free-flowing energy into the infinitesimally small droplet (*bindu*) at the centre of his heart *chakra*. When this is achieved, all conceptual thought automatically ceases. He has arrived at the goal of goals – bliss (*Mahamudra*).

Tantra and *Mahayana* in Tibet

Tibet is the highest country in the world. It is sparsely populated and covers an area of a million and a half square miles. Originally inhabited by a warlike, nomadic people of Mongol origin, speaking what has been called Tibeto-Burman, it sat crowning Asia in 'splendid isolation' for a millennium and a half – at least in the view of the imperial West – before beginning to reveal itself to the outside world during the nineteenth century. The British were the first to take an interest in it, sending military expeditions and political agents there. They were soon followed – not only by representatives of the other great powers but also by an army of European occultists and American Theosophists, who claimed it variously as Shangri-La, 'the forbidden land of the snows', the home of the secrets of past civilizations and the dwelling-place of immortal sages in possession of lost spiritual knowledge.

These outré wisdom-seekers were wrong, of course. In the first place, Tibet was not forbidden, for the Jesuits had set up shop there some centuries earlier, nor had it always been isolated. During a period of expansion, it had absorbed ideas and influences from everywhere around it, from India and China, from Iran and Central Asia – even from the shamans of Siberia. What it was, though, was essentially feudal. It was a tribally-oriented version of medieval Europe or Japan, set in its ways, with a culture firmly rooted in ancient tradition. Preserved within it, free from any effects of modernization, was its central religion: a mixture of *Mahayana* and Tantric Buddhism. This had survived in a form very like that in which it had existed centuries before in the Buddhic motherland of India. After the Chinese invasion of Tibet and the diaspora of many of Tibet's people, including lamas (gurus), it is the form of Buddhism which is most widely encountered in the West.

The early history of Tibet need not detain us long. It seems to have been consolidated into a kingdom in the early seventh century AD, when it began a period of military conquest. Up to that point, its religion had been essentially animist, presided over by a spell-casting shamanic priesthood called the *bon-po*. Then, some time in the seventh century, a king called Songtsen Gampo – by tradition an incarnation of the Bodhisattva Avalokiteshvara – sent an emissary south to Kashmir to develop a Tibetan alphabet and script. A century or so later, another king, Trisong Detsen, ordered the translation of a number of Buddhist texts from Chinese and Indian sources and also invited the first monks into the country, among them a Tantric Indian wonder-worker called Padmasambhava. Padmasambhava, it is said, subdued and co-opted to Buddhism all the local gods and demons. He helped build Tibet's first monastic complex at Samye and founded the sect of the *Nyingmapa* (Ancient Ones), which still survives to this day.

This early period is marked by what seems to have been a bitter, and sometimes murderous struggle between Buddhism and the popular animism of the *bon-po*, backed by most of the king's court.

Part Two: Buddhism after Buddha

One event stands out, though – a Great Debate held in the presence of King Ralpachen at the Samye monastery, between 793 and 794 pitted Indian Buddhist pandits against a leader of the Chinese Chan school of instant enlightenment. (It is likely to have featured the sort of ritualized gestures and elaborate forms of address still used in debate by Tibetan lamas.) The Indian gradualists seem to have won the day in this drawn-out battle between the two traditions and thirty years later a special commission of Tibetan and Indian scholars began standardizing the translations of Buddhist texts from Sanskrit – from then on the language from which virtually all Tibetan texts were taken. Precise equivalents for Sanskrit technical terms were established for present and future use and the result is a literature that remains internally consistent – and remarkably faithful to Sanskrit originals – today.

It was not long, however, before the newly-established *Sangha* ran foul of court intrigues. Ralpachen was murdered and Buddhism was ruthlessly suppressed for over a hundred and fifty years, only being kept alive by refugee monks and wandering *yogin*. The kingdom fell into chaos and it was not until the establishment of more or less stable independent governments in western, eastern and central Tibet around the year 1000 that the faith was allowed to return. Tibetans – among them a celebrated translator and (later) builder of monasteries, Rinchen Sangpo – began to travel to India, either to collect texts, to study with Tantric masters and at Buddhist universities, or to sit at the feet of adepts in their hermitages: as a man called Marpa did in Bihar.

Famous Indian teachers, one of them a legend called Atisa, made the journey in the reverse direction – northwards across the formidable Himalaya mountains. Atisa created the system of chronology still in use in Tibet, which defines each year by its position in a sixty-year cycle. The cycle relies on the combination of five

176

elements (earth, iron, water, wood and fire) with the twelve animals of the zodiac (dog, boar, mouse, ox, tiger, hare, dragon, serpent, horse, sheep, monkey and bird). Without Atisa's system, the writing of history – a later speciality among Tibetans, one of whom, Buston, wrote a definitive *History of Buddhism in India and Tibet* in the early fourteenth century – would have been more or less impossible.

With the help of this cross-fertilization of pilgrims and scholars, monasteries were soon restored; temples and new monasteries were built; and individual schools began to emerge, each favouring particular teachings and texts with their own special emphasis and style. At the same time, because of royal patronage, the *Sangha* as a whole became more and more wealthy and powerful and it was not long before it found itself at the core of the country's political life. By the time Buddhism was destroyed in India by the ruthless suppression of Muslim invaders, Tibet, in its fastness, had developed into a Buddhocracy in which the faith, the *Sangha* and the state had become one. Preserved in a time capsule, the Buddhism of medieval India survived with little or no alteration. Although there is a vast ancillary literature in the Tibetan language – commentaries, histories, biographies and verses – it contains almost nothing by way of new doctrine.

Instead, the received teachings were systematically analyzed and codified in the early period and by the fourteenth century – supervised by the remarkable historian Buston – they achieved their final, canonical form. There were two categories – the *Kangyur* (the *Vinaya*, *Sutras* and *Tantras*) and the *Tengyur* – made up of treatises, commentaries and various works on such related subjects as grammar, astrology and medicine. The *Kangyur* was first printed in Peking in 1411 and the whole Canon, all 330 or so volumes of it, was printed at Narthang in Tibet in the first half of the eighteenth century.

The Main Schools of Tibetan Buddhism

Kadampa ('Bound by Command'): This school – the first to have a clear and accepted historical origin – was founded by a lay disciple of the immigrant Indian teacher Atisa and it regarded a severe monastic discipline as a vital prerequisite for Tantric practice. The Dalai Lama has written about the members of this school, as quoted (in an amended form) in John Snelling's *The Buddhist Handbook*:

> Their trademark was this synthesis of various vehicles (yanas), as expressed by their saying, 'The external practice is moral discipline [i.e. Hinayanan obedience to the Vinaya]; the inner practice is the bodhi-mind [i.e. Mahayanan mysticism]; and practiced in secret, is the secret mantra [i.e. Vajrayanan Tantra].' In the Kadampa Order, these three were taken as interconnected, intersupportive aspects of training.

Sakya: This school, named for its principal monastery in southern Tibet, devolves from the teachings of Drogmi (992–1072), who spent many years studying *Tantra* in India: he translated one of the school's basic texts, the *Hejavra Tantra*. Another key text for the school is *The Way and Its Fruit* (*Lam-dre*), by the ninth-century Indian adept Virupa, a conflation of Sutric and Tantric teaching into a course of training designed to produce Enlightenment in a single lifetime. Sakyapa clerics are permitted to marry and the headship of the school traditionally passes from uncle to nephew. (The forty-first *Sakya Trizin* now lives in exile.) Early heads of the school wielded considerable political power. One was appointed as the viceregent of the Mongol overlordship in Tibet in the thirteenth century and his nephew succeeded him as the prelate and plenipotentiary of Kublai Khan.

Subsequent Chinese claims to Tibet as a 'natural' part of China were based on this emperor-client relationship.

Kargyu ('Transmitted Command'): The line of this school is traced back to two Indian yogic adepts, Tilopa and Naropa. Marpa studied with Naropa, the Tibetan pilgrim and founder of the Kargyupa school; one of the school's most important texts is *The Six Yogas of Naropa*, which includes the yoga of the *bardo* (the intermediate state between death and rebirth) and mystic heat-yoga (*dumo*), a practical necessity for any seeker alone in his snow-bound hermitage. Marpa, on his return from India, refused to become a monk and had become instead an ordinary householder. He married a woman whom he called *Nairatmya* ('no-self'), and with whom he practiced erotic Hejavran *Tantra*. It is a feature of the Kargyu sect that it requires neither celibacy nor monkhood – even though it has built monasteries of its own.

Marpa's chief disciple and successor as head of the Kargyupa school, Milarepa, is the most popular saint and the greatest poet of Tibetan Buddhism. As a young man he practised black magic in order to take revenge on an uncle who had dispossessed his widowed mother. In terror however at the karmic repercussions of this, he became Marpa's devoted *chela*. For six years, Marpa put him through the spiritual wringer: for example, he forced him to build a tall tower, then knock it down and rebuild it time after time as an act of expiation. Finally, though, he granted him access to Buddhahood and from that time on, for the remaining thirty-nine years of his life, Milarepa lived as a hermit on the high Himalayas near the border with Nepal, wearing nothing but a cotton cloth and eating nothing but herbs (a diet that turned his skin green). His song-poems are full of the agonies and ecstasies of the ascetic life, the heady mountain atmosphere and the joy of the *Dharma*.

After the time of Milarepa's succession, the Kargyupa school split into four branches, one of which was introduced into Bhutan in the seventeenth century and remains the main form of Buddhism both there, in Ladakh and in other parts of the region. Another was much favoured by the Mongol and Ming emperors of China. But one further offshoot, the so-called Karma Kargyu school, is of special interest. This school had a considerable following in the eastern part of Tibet, from where the head of the order, the Karmapa (sometimes known as 'the Black Hat Lama'), would go on elaborate progresses through the country with a large armed guard. Successive Karmapas were appointed, not on any hereditary basis, but by means of a system unique to Tibet – one also found in a number of other schools. Before each Karmapa dies, that is to say, he leaves behind directions which, after an appropriate time, set up a search for a child in whom he – or rather his compassionate spirit – has been reborn. Such voluntary reincarnations are known as *tulku* and carry the title of *rinpoche* ('blessed one'). The sixteenth Karmapa, exiled to Sikkim in 1959, soon afterwards sent two 'blessed ones' to the West to spread the school's teachings: Chogyam Trungpa Rinpoche and Chuje Akong Rinpoche, who founded the first Tibetan Buddhist centre in Scotland.

Nyingma ('Old Ones'): Instituted, according to legend, by the wonder-worker Padmasambhava, 'Nyingma' was perhaps an umbrella term for all those who cleaved to, and carried through the dark years of chaos, the teachings and practices of the first monks to arrive in Tibet. The school was organized and given new life by Guru Choswang in the thirteenth century, when it began to build monasteries and gather together a new canon of its own, based on manuscripts, purportedly written by Padmasambhava, that it claimed to have discovered hidden in caves and other secret places. Since Padmasambhava was believed to be a manifestation of Avalokiteshvara –and the spiritual equal of the Sakyamuni Buddha – these were holy scriptures indeed. They were known as *termas* (treasures) and formed the second part of the Nyingmaka tradition, after *kamas* – the sayings of the original Indian masters. Many of the *termas* – for all the later suspicions about the convenience of their discovery – do seem in fact to be of considerable antiquity. One of them, the so-called *Tibetan Book of the Dead*, not only appears to record extremely ancient ideas about life after death but it also bears a strong similarity to Egyptian, Persian and early Christian writings on the subject.

Nyingmapa *lamas* never achieved the organized power of some of their rivals, largely because they were individualistic, typically married and working at a local level by providing magical services – exorcism, rain-making, divination, healing and so on – to ordinary Tibetans. Indeed, they took over many of the responsibilities, and some of the teachings, of the indigenous animist priesthood, the *bon-po*; and they never fully adopted repressive Buddhist morality. Instead, they lay stress on the central role played by the physical body and its passions in the search for enlightenment, arguing, as the Celestial Bodhisattva Samantabhadra does in one of their texts:

> Suchness, including yourself, is not intrinsically entangled - so why should you try to disentangle ourself? It is not intrinsically deluded – so why should you seek the truth apart from it?

Like the Chan school in China, they prefer intuitive insight to any carefully amassed knowledge; and like Indian Tantric masters of the early period, they follow a practice which consists, according to Conze, of the following:

1. the mental creation of tutelaries (*yidam*) with the help of mantras, visions and the 'sky walkers'.
2. the control of the occult body, with its arteries, semen, virility etc.
3. the realisation of the true nature of one's own mind.

They are also much preoccupied with the nature of death and rebirth and distinguish six intermediate states between normal awareness and the spiritual realm of *Nirvana*. Three of these are experienced by an 'ethereal' body in the interval between death and reconception, seen as lasting forty-nine days – and offering the sort of visions recorded in *The Book of the Dead*. Three others are experienced in the womb, in controlled dreaming and in deep trance.

Claims have been made that Nyingma represents Buddhism in its purest form. Indeed, in the shape of Dzogchen ('The Great Perfection') – a form of Nyingmapa tantric teaching popular in the West – it is seen as the essence of all other teachings, the basic core of Buddhist practice, striking right to the heart of the primordial state of being within us all.

Gelug ('Virtuous'): The key master of the Gelugpa sect – sometimes known as 'The Yellow Hat Order' in the West – was the scholar and reformer Tsongkhapa (1357–1419), also known as Je Rinpoche. Tsongkhapa, who is identified with Manjushri, the Celestial Bodhisattva of wisdom, was originally a member of the Kadampa school, but he soon gained a huge reputation as an independent teacher. After winning control of the central temple in Lhasa, he set up three monasteries near the holy city where he instituted a curriculum of doctrinal studies leading to the degree of *Geshe* ('spiritual friend'), a sort of doctorate of philosophy. He set great store by the long and careful study of the *Sutras* and of Indian masters such as Nagarjuna and Asanga; he was a champion of strict monastic discipline; and he condemned the use of worldly magic. The *Tantra*, he pronounced, should only be used for the pursuit of Enlightenment and in the sixteen volumes of his Collected Works he laid out the path to it as a series of graduated stages, either through the Mahayanist Six Perfections or through *Tantra*.

Tsongkhapa is important as a great synthesizer and re-energizer of the faith. He was, says Edward Conze, 'the last great thinker of the Buddhist world' and after his death he became the object of a religious cult of his own. His body was embalmed and enshrined in a *stupa* at one of his university-monasteries, Ganden, which was later invaded and violated by Chinese soldiers. The annual festival of Ngacho Chemno, when thousands of butter-lamps used to be burnt, is a commemoration of his death and he is also believed to have started the three-week-long 'Great Prayer' Festival, which used to be held annually in Lhasa immediately after the Tibetan New Year.

In the course of the fifteenth century, Gelugpa elders helped to stabilize the country over the long term by adopting the *tulku* system of succession. This was based on the old Mahayanan doctrine which held that Buddhas and Bodhisattvas could create phantom-bodies to do their work on earth (or in any other realm). The head of the Order, Gendrun-trup, was recognized as having been the creation of Avalokiteshvara. He was retrospectively declared the first Dalai (or 'Ocean') Lama and, from that time on, with the death of each Dalai Lama, a new child, conceived forty-nine days later, is searched for as the next phantom-body of the last patriarch-cum-Bodhisattva - all this being based on extremely complex rules laid down by the Congregation of Rites. His main palace in Lhasa, where he is educated under the direction of regents, is called Potala, after the dwelling-place of the Bodhisattva in southern India. A second, and historically rival,

183

authority within the school is the reincarnating Panchen Lama, whose traditional home is the monastic complex of Tashilhunpo in southern Tibet.

Despite the occasional warring between the followers of the two Lamas, the theocratic *tulku* system prevented any jockeying – or worse – for supreme power, which soon became the prerogative of the Dalai Lamas of the school. The third Lama converted the Mongols for the second time, co-opting their gods and demons in the process, it is said, as protectors of the *Dharma*. The fourth was actually the grandson of the Mongol Khan; and the sixth, a great scholar, was installed by Gusri Khan as the virtual ruler of Tibet under Mongol protection in 1642. The new Manchu dynasty in China confirmed his position, and relied on him and his successors to keep Tibet peaceful and protective of its interests.

The system broke down once, during the rule of the sixth Dalai Lama, who was accused of degeneracy, perhaps because he tried to revive erotic *Tantra*. There was bitter infighting among the Gelugpa lamas, and a Mongol army had to intervene. After that time, though a delicate political balance was by and large maintained, with successive Dalai Lamas and their regents providing social stability and continuity and managing at the same time to keep the Chinese from meddling in the country's internal affairs and establishing a presence. In this way, conditions favouring the religious life were preserved; militarism was reduced to a minimum; animals were protected; and noise and unrest were suppressed. For 450 years Tibet became a Buddhocracy for Buddhism reached into every corner of Tibetan life, even if slowly but surely ossifying in the process. In 1885, a visitor reported that monks and nuns made up a fifth of the Tibetan population: There were seven hundred and sixty thousand of them in eighteen hundred monasteries.

It was only, in fact, with the coming of the twentieth century that life in Tibet began to change radically for the first time in centuries. The thirteenth Dalai Lama was forced to leave the country twice, first in 1904 (for Mongolia) after a massacre by a British expeditionary force, and secondly in 1910 (for India) when another army – this time Chinese – invaded. He returned in 1913 after the fall of the Manchu dynasty and between then and his death in 1933 he led Tibet through a period of more or less full independence, during which he did his best to prepare Tibetans for the coming onrush of the modern world. Inevitably, he was resisted by conservatives in the monastic community, who not only opposed change of any kind, but had no conception of what life was like beyond the country's borders. They found out in 1950, when the fourteenth Dalai Lama was still only fifteen and recently enthroned. For modernity arrived in Tibet with a vengeance in the shape of an occupying Chinese Communist army. Nine years later, during a general uprising against the Chinese, the Dalai Lama fled to India where, as a figure of great spiritual authority, he now lives in exile in the hill-station of Dharamsala.

Ways and Means in Tantric Buddhism

Of absolutely central importance to Tantric Buddhism is the relationship between the *siddha* (adept) and his *chela* (disciple or student). The *siddha* is sometimes referred to in Tantric texts as Buddhism's 'Fourth Jewel', being of equal importance to the 'Three Jewels' of Buddha, *Sangha* and *Dharma*. Tantric practices are said to be useless without his guidance and blessing, and the *chela* is required to give him absolute submission and devotion as the embodiment of Buddha. This has been compared to a patient placing himself obediently, when ill, in the hands of a skilled surgeon: but in traditional lamaism the process of 'giving up' went further. For whatever the *chela* owned was seen as the personal property of his *guru*.

Siddhas are by no means always monks. They came, and come, from any walk of life and caste. They do menial work and very often flout the conventions of more orthodox believers. Their status as outsiders highlights the fact that in *Vajrayana* every form of human activity is seen as an expression of Buddha nature and every situation as an opportunity to cultivate the enlightened mind. It is not the task of the *siddha* to reform his students but to show them that enlightened energy is already manifest in their make-up and behaviour, however neurotic and passion-contaminated they may be. Everything is capable of transformation: anger into intelligence, ignorance into equanimity, passion into compassion and loving kindness. Not even sexual desire and pleasure are seen as enemies of spirituality. As the sixth Dalai Lama said:

> If one's thoughts towards the Dharma were of the same intensity as those towards love, one would become a Buddha in this very body, in this very life.

The enemies of spirituality, in sex as everywhere else in human life, are the attachment and greed of the fictitious 'self' which puts personal gratification before the needs of others.

Tantric practices are usually classified under four headings – Action, Performance, Yoga and Highest (or Supreme) *Tantra* – which are designed to fit the different needs and abilities of individual seekers, who have to find the level appropriate to them. Even then, it is not for everyone to follow the Tantric path, despite the fact that it holds out the possibility of achieving Enlightenment within a single lifetime. Aspirants, first of all, should already have accumulated enough merit – through good works, moral restraint, patience and so on, in this and previous lives – to be able to control their passions and transform the experiences of everyday life, rather than retreat from them into asceticism in the Hinayana-Mahayanan manner. They should also have some skill in meditation, an understanding of Emptiness and, above all, a commitment to follow the path, not for selfish personal betterment, but for the benefit of others. Compassion must be their essential guiding light.

Their next step is to find – and make what is called 'dharmic connection' – with a *guru*. To teach the lower categories of *Tantra*, he (or she) does not have to be a fully enlightened practitioner, but he must have the expertise to be able to judge whether his *chela* is ready and has the necessary qualities to be able to follow the Tantric path. He must protect him from pitfalls and dangers along the way, and steer him towards those practices which will be most beneficial in his particular case.

Once the two-way commitment has been made between *chela* and *guru*, the *chela* will be initiated into the alternative reality of his chosen deity's *mandala* through the ceremony of the *abhisheka* ritual. This is a public event which is open to all believers, but to the serious Tantric inititiate it represents both a giving of collective permission and a gathering of power to be stored up for the way ahead. From this point on, he can receive teachings and begin to gather the provisions for the journey onward in the form of ethical behaviour, purity, right thinking and correct motivation.

At the level of Action Tantra, he is now required to pay intense devotional respect to his chosen deity: to recite *mantras* and prayers, to make offerings and to perform *mudras* and acts of obeisance, including what is known as 'the hundred thousand prostrations'. At the same time – or at a later stage – he will practise Guru Yoga in order to strengthen his devotion to, and reliance on, his lama-guide as the incarnation of his deity. Closer and closer identification with both *guru* and deity will ultimately involve a direct transmission of the state of enlightened mind from teacher to student – and with it the final understanding that the search is not for something outside in the world, but for what is within.

It will also involve the ability to generate an alternative *mandala*-world, populated by deities, via mantras and meditation. In a typical visualization, the devotee envisions himself as the Buddha-deity at the heart of this *mandala*-realm, inhabiting a 'divine house' or interior castle much like that conjured in meditation by the medieval Spanish mystic, St. Teresa of Avila. In Highest Tantra, the initiate learns to summon the deity from the primal Emptiness of mind or from his essence distilled in the seed-syllable (*bija*), and so becomes ready for the final actualization stage, at which full identification and dissolution of self takes place.

Chapter Eight:

Buddhism Throughout the World

The Death of Buddhism in the Indian Heartland

The conventional wisdom is that Buddhism disappeared from India in around 1200 AD because of its ruthless suppression by Muslim invaders, who were determined to root out every last trace of what they saw as idolatry; and it is certainly true that the new Turkic conquerors burned down Buddhist monasteries and butchered Buddhist monks whenever and wherever they found them. The great university at Nalanda, for example, was razed in 1198. When a Tibetan pilgrim visited it thirty-seven years later, all he found was an old monk teaching Sanskrit grammar to a handful of students in the ruins.

This is by no means the whole of the story, though. For Hinduism and Jainism were also suppressed and with equal brutality – and yet both somehow managed to survive. In those parts of the country that were untouched by the Muslim invasion furthermore, in Nepal and south India, for example Buddhism also died away, although rather more slowly. The truth seems to be that Buddhism on the sub-continent, even before the conquest, was already played out as a spiritual force. It had lost its roots in the rural population; and it had come to rely more and more on royal and aristocratic patronage. Once that had been lost – and its social base had been destroyed – it no longer had much to offer ordinary people. Jainists, by contrast – less visible as targets than saffron-robed Buddhist monks – probably survived because there was continuing popular support for ascetics, especially among wealthy merchants. Brahminism, for its part - for all its own great temples and monasteries - remained part of the social fabric of every village, taking care, as it did, of all the rites Buddhism had ceded to it: those of the agricultural cycle, and of birth, marriage and death.

Two other factors, however, also played a role. The first was that, over the preceding centuries, there had been a gradual erosion of the lines that had separated Buddhism and Brahminic Hinduism. The Buddha and a number of Buddhist deities had been absorbed into the Hindu pantheon; the *Vedas* were formally taught at the Buddhist university at Nalanda; and Buddhist Tantras had their precise counterparts in Brahminic literature, which refer constantly to Mahayanan deities. The iconographies and mythologies of the two religions – even their teachings – had become more and more like each other. There were fewer and fewer creative disagreements between them. So it was easy enough for the under-appreciated Buddhist lay community simply to transfer its allegiance, without much discomfort, when hard times came.

The second factor was that Buddhism had never had any particular allegiance to place – the lamp of the *Dharma*, after all, could be lit and maintained anywhere. So while the less flexible and internationally-minded Brahminists and Jainists stood their ground at home, the Buddhist monks who survived the onslaught of militant Islam simply moved elsewhere: to Nepal, for example Tibet and China. On the Indian subcontinent, the wellspring of creative energy that had renewed Buddhism twice in the past had finally dried up. That energy now lay elsewhere.

Buddhism Beyond the Borders

By this time, of course, Buddhism was already well established in Southeast Asia, having been brought there by early Indian settlers and traders. Burma, for instance, which received its first Buddhist missionaries in the third century BC, seems from the first to have been dominated by the devout *Theravada* form of Buddhism, imported from Ceylon. Later though it fell under Mahayanist influence, and it seems to have been dominated in the ninth century AD by a powerful organization of *Vrijnaya* monks called Aris ('Aryans' or 'nobles') who practised *Tantra,* made use of spells and animal sacrifices and worshipped the Mahayanan pantheon.

Two hundred years later though a fresh supply of *Theravada* monks (and scriptures) were brought in from Ceylon by royal order and although the *Mahayana* influence persisted in art and literature for at least another four hundred years, *Theravada* Buddhism eventually took over completely in the 1490s as, in effect, the state religion. Pagan, until it was destroyed by the Mongols at the end of the thirteenth century, was the most important Buddhist centre in the country, said to have been home to 9,000 pagodas and temples (among them the famous Ananda Temple). In the fourteenth century, the celebrated 326-feet-high Shwedagon pagoda was built in Rangoon as a gigantic reliquary for some of the Buddha's hair.

Cambodia (now Kampuchea), Thailand and Laos followed more or less similar paths. Cambodia, on the main trade route between India and China, was already throughly Indianised by the fourth century AD; and under an Indian ruling house and priesthood it developed a syncretic religion in which *Mahayana* Buddhism and Brahminism played more or less equal parts. At the beginning of the ninth century, this was taken over by the newly unified Khmer kingdom at Angkor, with its capital and marvellous temples. But Theravada Buddhism once more supervened four hundred years later – just as the Thai and Lao people were beginning to form states of their own in the area – brought in by a missionary Burmese monk. It was ultimately accepted by the kings of all three peoples and became the state religion, with various lingering traces of Brahminism and indigenous cults. In Thailand, for example – which has produced some of the finest bronze images of the Buddha in history – the King is styled 'the protector of the *Dharma*' and Buddhism has infiltrated every corner of the nation's life. Yet, as in Burma (now Nyangmai), petitions are still made to local genii and tree spirits, rather than the Buddha.

In Indonesia – also more or less completely Indianised by the fifth century AD – Sumatra became Theravadan, while Java followed the early Cambodian pattern. Both Brahminism and Buddhism took hold there in forms that harmonized with pre-existing magical and animist practices – Brahminism in the form of Shiva-worship and Buddhism in its *Mahayana* form, with *Tantra* as the link between them. The Sailendra kings filled the island's central plain with beautifully sculpted temples: including Borobodur, the largest and most remarkable example in southern Asia. This great ninth-century monument, which boasts 27,000 square feet of carvings and over 500 stone Buddhas, is a giant *mandala*, representing both the Buddhic cosmos, centred around Mount Meru, and the spiritual journey taken from *samsara* towards *nirvana*. Present-day pilgrims, as in the past, climb upwards on a path that leads through a succession of five terraces. Reliefs depicting the life of Sakyamuni and stories from the

Jakata and *Mahayana* scriptures can be seen along the way. When the pilgrims finally arrive at the top terrace they encounter three ascending circles of *stupas*, with the *stupa* symbolizing both mountain and the apprehension of Emptiness rising in the middle.

Fifty years after Borobodur was built, another Sailendra king erected a further great temple nearby, this time to Shiva. (Both may in fact have been funerary monuments representing their different paths to salvation.) Increasingly in fact, as time went on, the distinctions between the two religions faded, and a cult of *Shiva-Buddha*, with strong magical and Tantric elements emerged , mostly dedicated to the redemption of the souls of the dead. This produced, in thirteenth-century Java, some of the most beautiful of all Buddhist sculptures, in which kings and queens were represented as Celestial Buddhas or the Perfection of Wisdom and so on. But it was largely suppressed in the fifteenth century, – as was *Theravada* in Sumatra by a fresh wave of Muslim conquerors .

In all of these Southeast Asian countries, Buddhism has survived in one form or another until the present day, although it was recently almost totally destroyed in Laos and Cambodia by the Pathet Lao and Khmer Rouge respectively. In Bali, and elsewhere in Indonesia, Buddhism is still manifest in surviving forms of mystic Hindu-Buddhism and can be felt in the popular appeasement of dead spirits and ancestor worship. In Burma, eighty per cent or so of the population remain Buddhist; and every layman becomes a novice for a while, receiving some education in the monasteries. In Thailand, where an even higher percentage of Thais are Buddhist, and there is a Buddhist king, the *wats* (monasteries) also play an important role in education and social cohesion; and *Theravada* has survived in an especially pure and ascetic form in the northeast of the country in the so-called Forest Tradition (much admired in the West). It is not surprising that Thai monks were repeatedly summoned back to the mother country of Ceylon during its long years of European rule, in order to re-seed and bring back to life the local *Theravada Sangha* whenever it showed signs of collapsing.

What none of these Southeast Asian countries were to produce, however, was any revivification of the Buddhist *Sangha* as a whole. The monks of the *Theravada* tradition continued to be concerned with maintaining orthodoxy and preserving the Buddha's teachings in as pure a form as possible, while those following *Mahayana* and *Tantra* proved only too successful at adapting themselves to purely local needs and practices. None of the monks, that is to say, produced any new speculative literature or brought about revolution in either doctrine or approach. Such innovation had to come from a place in which, finally free from constrictive Indian models, Buddhism could adapt into a new form that was expressive of the national character: China.

Chinese Forms of Buddhism

At the end of the sixth century AD, China was once more united into a single empire, first under the Sui dynasty (581–618) and then under the T'ang (618–907). Thus began what might be called the golden age of Buddhism in China. A number of clearly defined schools arose, nearly all of them of Indian origin and based upon intense study of particular Sanskrit texts, but becoming more and more Chinese in outlook and philosophical cast as time went by. Many of these subsequently ebbed away, in part because of the dissolution of the monasteries ordered (and later revoked) by imperial edict in 845, when Buddhist institutions were destroyed, their lands and wealth confiscated, and their monks and nuns ordered to return to secular life. By that time, however, a number of them had already been exported to Japan, where they were further developed. They are worth mentioning here.

The Mantra or Tantric School (Mi-Tsung) consisted of devotees of the *Mahavairocana* (or 'Great Brilliance') *Sutra,* and it was for a time highly favoured by eighth-century T'ang rulers because of its magic powers and occult control over cosmic forces. It was later supplanted at court by Tibetan *lamas* – who built the famous 'Lamaist Cathedral' in Peking – but it re-emerged in Japan as Shingon.

The Avatamsaka or 'Flower Wreath' School (Hua-Yen) focused on the *Avatamsaka Sutra*, one of the scriptures of the Yogacarans, claiming it to be the most uncompromising expression of the Buddha's teachings. Avatamsakans held that everything in the cosmos interpenetrated everything else, so everything and anything in it, even the smallest particle of dust, was an equal expression of the harmony of Totality. All things were One. Thus Oneness was in all things and all things were equally worthy as objects of meditation. The bias of the school was towards contemplation and aesthetic appreciation (unlike the interventionist Tantra School), and it greatly influenced the Chinese attitude to nature, inspiring many artists in China and later in Japan, where it was known as Kegon.

The T'ien-t'ai or White Lotus School (Fa-hua) was named after Mount T'ien-t'ai, the home of its most important early patriarch, Chih-i (538–597). It followed the Avatamsaka school by maintaining that the mundane and the spiritual were not separate, but one – although it arrived at this conclusion from a slightly different philosophical perspective. Its central scripture was the *White Lotus of the True Law*

Sutra, and it represents an attempt to synthesize and harmonize all *Mahayana* Buddhist doctrines. The idea of harmony (as against dissension and dissonance) was very dear to the Chinese.; by bringing order to seemingly contradictory teachings, stressing that the ineffable was omnipresent in ordinary life and allowing that every being in the world possessed the Buddha-nature, the school was not only popular with ordinary people but also with the ruling classes, who saw it as promoting social order. In its doctrine it gave practitioners plenty of leeway for individual choice; and, in its practice, it laid equal stress on concentration (*chi*) and insight (*kuan*), the flash of intuition that suddenly penetrates to the heart of Ultimate Reality. In the end, the T'ien-t'ai School in China became a victim of its own efforts to be all things to all men. It promoted a syncretization of Buddhism with Confucianism; and the neo-Confucianism that was the result destroyed it. It survived in Japan as Tendai.

The Pure Land School (Ching-t'u) was of a different order from any of the above; and even though it produced no great masters after the ninth century, it was to have a pervasive influence on developments within Chinese Buddhism long after that. The Pure Land had its roots in the notion – also widespread in India – that a degenerate period would set in a thousand or so years after the death of the Sakyamuni Buddha, one in which it would become increasingly difficult to achieve Enlightenment through personal effort alone. (Unmediated personal effort, indeed, could be regarded as egoistic and presumptuous.) Another source was the common early practice of meditative concentration upon the Celestial Buddhas of the ten directions, of whom Amithaba, the Buddha of the Pure Land or Western Paradise (Sukhavati), was one. The main scriptural focus for the School was a first century AD Sanskrit text, the *Sukhavativyuha*, which claimed to tell Amithaba's story. One of the things it recorded was that as the Bodhisattva Dharmakara, inconceivable numbers of aeons ago, Amithaba had made forty-eight vows, including one that promised that anyone who called on his name would be saved. He had later become the Buddha Amithaba and, in keeping with his earlier vows, he had established the Pure Land or Western Paradise for those who invoked him.

In the Pure Land School, therefore, meditation took second place to the *mantra*-like repetition of the Buddha's name (*O-mi-to-fo*), and devotion to Amithaba took every form: sculpture, painting, hymns and the constant reproduction of the *Smaller* and *Larger Sukhavativyuha Sutras*. And because the veneration of Amithaba coincided, roughly speaking, with the popular Taoist notion of a spirit or spirits who kept a record of everyone's actions – and adjusted the length of their lives or granted them immortality accordingly – Pure Land had many Taoist converts. The first Pure Land master, T'an-luan (476–542) had been a Taoist himself, as we have seen, and he further widened access to the Amithaba cult by declaring that even the worst of sinners, except those who had blasphemed against the *Dharma*, could be reborn in the Western Paradise. All they had to have was faith.

The Pure Land School, then, was anything but élitist. It was both practical and democratic; and though, in its later development, it came to stress morality, meditation and scholarship as important further vehicles towards salvation, it continued to appeal to all classes in society with its message about the worth of every individual, wrapped – whatever his caste or position – in the boundless love of Amithaba. In its heyday it attracted everyone from emperors to slaves, including scholars, artists, soldiers, peasants, women, monks and novices; and though it was later condemned as being 'vulgar' and 'foreign' by *comme-il-faut* neo-Confucians, its influence remained, being transmitted into Japan in the form of the Jodo and Jodo Shin sub-schools. Although Pure Land also introduced a cult of the Indian Celestial Bodhisattva Avalokiteshvara – transformed ultimately into a female deity called Kuanyin – 'no native Chinese god', in the words of Robinson and Johnson in their *The Buddhist Religion*, 'has ever commanded the universal worship that [Amito] has received'.

Ch'an

All of the schools discussed above, particularly T'ien-t'ai and Pure Land, represented the adaptation of Buddhist ideas and doctrines to a specifically Chinese environment, both spiritual and social. None of them, though, had the lasting impact of a further school, the Dhyana (or 'Meditation') School, which was known in Chinese as Ch'an (Korean: *Son*; Japanese: *Zen*). Ch'an, in fact, represents the last great turn of the wheel in the development of Buddhist thought after *Abhidharma*, *Mahayana* and *Tantra* and it gave a new kind of saint to Buddhism, who was the successor of the *arhant*, the *bodhisattva* and the *siddha*: the *roshi* (or Ch'an 'master').

Ch'an represented a sort of back-to-basics movement within the Buddhist establishment. It held that all the paraphernalia of Chinese monastic practice and doctrine (the lectures on philosophy; the constant reading of the *Sutras* and commentaries; the codes of behaviour; the devotional rituals; the use of images; the constant pressure to perform good works; and so on) ran the risk of obscuring, rather than pointing the way to, Enlightenment – the one and only true goal. What it proposed was a radical simplification of the means used to achieve what remained the heart of the matter – the direct insight which had transformed Sakyamuni into the Buddha under the Bodhi tree. It announced that salvation could not be achieved through the study of books; it had to be practically realized. It brought the discipline of meditation, that's to say, right back centre-stage.

In doing so, Ch'an claimed to be part of a special transmission that was 'outside the scriptures', beyond words and writing, a transmission that had originally come from the Sakyamuni Buddha himself. On one occasion, thousands of people went to hear him preach at Vulture Mountain and for some time he sat before them in silence. Then he held up a flower. Only one person there, a seeker called Mahakashyapa understood what he meant – that words were no substitute for the living organism – and at that moment he intuited the whole essence of Buddha's teaching. The first transmission between mind and mind, acknowledged by Sakyamuni and Mahakashyapa with a complicit smile, had taken place.

This transmission from mind to mind and from master to student had then continued in India, according to Ch'an traditions, until it was brought to China by its twenty-eighth recipient, a south Indian monk called Bodhidharma, in about AD 470. Bodhidharma was said to have spent nine years contemplating a wall after his arrival and even to have cut off his eyelids so that his gaze would not falter. At some point, however, he found time to meet the pious Emperor Wu of Liang. Their conversation, in the version given by Jane Hope and Borin Van Loon in *Buddha for Beginners*, is fairly typical of Ch'an exchanges:

> 'From the beginning of my reign I have built many temples, translated numerous scriptures and supported the monastic life. What merits have I earned?'
> 'None'.
> 'Why?'
> 'All these are inferior deeds. A true deed of merit comes straight from the heart and is not concerned with worldly achievements.'

'Then what is your holy doctrine all about?'

'Vast emptiness, nothing holy'.

'Then who are you?'

'I don't know'.

Bodhidharma, who is conventionally pictured as a wild, exophthalmic and bushy-bearded barbarian, became the legendary First Patriarch of the Ch'an school, and he passed the robe (and the transmission) on to his disciple, Hui-k'o – although not before Hui-k'o had been severely tested. When he first asked for teaching, Bodhidharma made him stand outside in the snow until the drifts came up to his knees. Finally, desperate to demonstrate his earnestness, Hui-k'o, according to the story, cut off one of his arms with his sword. At last the master was impressed, and ushered him in.

'My soul isn't at peace', Hui-k'o is supposed to have said. 'Please pacify it, master'.

'Bring your soul here and I'll pacify it for you', replied Bodhidharma.

'I've been looking for it for years but haven't been able to find a trace of it'.

'There!' said Bodhidharma with a gesture. 'It's pacified once and for all!'

Bodhidharma had obviously absorbed from the *Tao* some of its earthiness and irreverent humour, and his successors, from Hui-k'o onwards, seem to have taught an ascetic form of Tao-Buddhism. It is not, in fact, until the time of the Fifth Patriarch, that Ch'an as an independent school of thought begins to come into focus – even through via what may be later propoganda. A tale records that the Patriarch announced that before he died he would pass on his mantle to the disciple who could write a verse that best expressed the true nature of Enlightenment. One of them, a sophisticated and learned monk called Shen-hsui (608?–708), his chief disciple, wrote:

> The body is the Bhodi tree,
> The mind is like a bright mirror in a stand.
> Take care to wipe it constantly
> And allow no dust to cling.

But another disciple, an ex-woodcutter and lowly monastery menial called Hui-neng (638–713), thought he could do better. He wrote, in a kind of gloss:

> Fundamentally the Bodhi tree does not exist;
> The bright mirror also has no stand.
> Since everything is primordially empty,
> What is there for dust to cling to?

The story goes that when the Patriarch read this he interviewed Hui-neng at the dead of night, recognized that he had been truly awoken to Enlightenment, and passed on his robe to him in secret. This not only broke every rule of monastic law but it also officially, so to speak, downgraded book-learning in favour of direct apprehension. (Ch'an later came to dismiss the complex cosmological and psychological theories of other schools as 'rubbish' and 'useless furniture'.) More than that, because Shen-hsui was identified with the so-called northern school of Ch'an, which held that Enlightenment could only be gradually achieved by purification and strenuous practice (the constant wiping of the mirror), it was abandoned by mainstream Ch'an in favour of the teachings of the southern school, represented by Hui-neng. A central belief of the latter school was that since all beings were already part of the emptiness of Buddha-nature, they therefore did not need purifying. Enlightenment could be achieved in a single instant.

The whole story of the competition between Hui-neng and Shen-hsui may well have been a later confection of the victorious southern school. But it also contains another element that was very important to the development of Ch'an – the interview, at the dead of night, between the Patriarch and Hui-neng. Interviews like this, between master and disciple, became a crucial adjunct to meditation and more or less standard practice in Ch'an, the aim of which was 'to cultivate no-thought' without self-assertion, striving or, indeed, deliberate purpose – the ground-base onto which Enlightenment could be encouraged to supervene. Such interviews enabled the master to check on a disciple's spiritual progress in general. But they also provided an opportunity to provoke insight or awareness (Chinese: *wu*; Japanese: *satori*) – a shift to a higher level of understanding which was sometimes equated with Enlightenment itself. Robinson and Johnson, in their *The Buddhist Religion*, explain the process:

> Dialogs that occur in these private encounters form a substantial part of later Ch'an literature. They are terse, often witty, sometimes bizarre and obscure. The master usually had a lot of students, and only two or three short periods a day were set aside for interviews, so the chance was precious. In addition, the student's hopes and fears were usually keyed up by long waiting and intense striving, so that the meeting had the sudden death quality of a duel. The master diagnoses the student's problem and treats it. Sometimes he simply explains or advises. Sometimes he provokes, shocks, or otherwise manipulates the student.

The Ch'an strategy is to catch a person at the critical moment and do the appropriate thing that triggers awakening. Chan masters similarly treat each case as sui generis, acting and expecting responses with spontaneity and without preconceptions or premeditation.

Any and all means were appropriate in this 'treatment', including suddenly beating the students with a stick, slapping their faces or tweaking their noses, or making rude or inconsequential noises. But one of the most powerful tools was what came to be called the *kung-an* (Japanese: *koan*). The *kung-an* (roughly speaking, 'legal precedent or authority') was in practice a riddle or seemingly nonsensical remark, usually connected with a saying or action of one of the Ch'an masters. (A variety of these *kung-ans* were collected in *Sayings of the Ancient Worthies*.) Some are more or less comprehensible, as in this story of Pai-chang and his student Ling-yu, also recorded in Robinson and Johnson:

> When Ling-yu was twenty-three, he came to Pai-chang, who recognized his talent and took him as an attendant. One day the master said, 'Who's there?'
> 'It's Ling-yu.'
> 'Poke and see whether there's still some fire in the stove.'
> Ling-yu poked around and said, 'There's no fire.'
> Pai-chang got up, went to the stove, poked quite a bit, managed to stir up a small glow, and said to his pupil, 'Isn't this fire?' Ling-yu was awakened, knelt down, and bowed in gratitude to the master.

Pai-chang was not only telling Ling-yu that he wasn't striving hard enough. He was also pointing towards the nature of ultimate reality, the direct experience of the unextinguished – and inextinguishable – fire within.

Other *kung-ans* made less immediate sense – as this, recorded as an interview between Hui-neng and one of his disciples, shows. The disciple asked Hui-neng: 'How do I get rid of ignorance?'

'Cease running after things', he replied. 'Stop thinking about what is right and wrong. Just see, at this very moment, what your original face was like before your mother and father were born.'

Another *kung-an*, quoted in Conze, takes the form of a three-line stanza:

> In the square pool there is a turtle-nosed serpent.
> Ridiculous indeed when you come to think of it!
> Who pulled out the serpent's head?

The purpose of the *kung-an*, however absurd, was to point the way towards ultimate reality. This was in the end inexpressible, but Ch'an masters were not content with simply saying this by evolving methods of what Conze calls 'stating it through a non-statement'. Put another way, we are so accustomed to the existence of rational answers to our questions that we must be put through the shock of facing the fact that there is no answer at all to this central question. The whole intellectual apparatus of mind has to be violently short-circuited if we are to find our own answer and experience reality directly. The beauty of the language of *kung-an* – known as 'strange words and stranger actions' – is that it is not remotely scholastic. Instead, it is an acting-out and an off-the-cuff invocation of objects in the world that is designed to jolt or deflect the mind of an individual student in the right direction. It is, if you like, the Buddha-mind of the master speaking directly, beyond the power of any mere words, to the Buddha-mind that inhabits his pupil.

As a result of this – because each interview, each jolt and deflection, was so to speak tailor-made – we know little of Ch'an teaching practice as a whole since its masters, distrusting words as another kind of attachment, wrote little down. Indeed, beyond sermons, some hymns and collections of cryptic sayings and anecdotes, there is little that can be described as Ch'an literature at all. This raises a number of questions, both about the status of the masters and about the very nature of Ch'an Enlightenment.

It is natural to suppose that the Ch'an master, like the Tibetan *siddha*, was regarded as the very embodiment of Buddha by his disciples. The Ch'an Patriarchs, indeed, are referred to as 'venerable Buddhas' and a collection of sermons by the (perhaps mythical) Hui-neng is deliberately entitled a *Sutra*, a word usually reserved for the Sakyamuni Buddha's teachings. What their realization as Buddhas consisted in, though, is a very much harder question to answer. For the word for Enlightenment in Ch'an texts is not the word *pu-ti*, applied to Sakyamuni's Enlightenment, but once again *wu* ('insight' or 'awareness'); and it seems to have consisted in the simple cessation of all ambition, all striving – much closer to Taoist ideals than those of traditional Buddhism.

Meditation is central to this achievement in Ch'an, in that it produces in initiates via constant introspection an inner potentiatily: a state of 'being in thought, yet devoid of thought', a state in which the mind 'stops dashing hither and thither'. Then comes the moment of 'sudden' enlightenment, in which this 'inner potentiality' breaks through into ordinary consciousness and all doubts and problems instantaneously drop away. From this point on, the enlightened initiate continues to engage fully with the world, but he is no longer completely of it. He exists in an eternal present, beyond birth, death, space and time. In the words of Hai-yun: 'To eat all day yet not to swallow a grain of rice; to walk all day yet not tread an inch of ground; to have no distinction during that time between object and subject; and to be inseparable from things all day long, yet not be deluded by them – this is to be the man who is at ease in himself.'

The approach to Ch'an Enlightenment, in other words, may involve complex and arduous preparation, but its achievement is simplicity itself. It can be achieved anywhere, as one contemporary Buddhist has put it: 'working in the fields, cooking rice, hearing one's name called, a slap, a kick!' There is no essential difference between the sacred and the profane, as Ch'an monastic practice had already established in the eighth century. (Po-Chang, also known as Huai-hai, had decreed that Ch'an monks, unlike others, should work. 'A day without work', he announced, 'is a day without food'.) Enlightenment was therefore fully open to lay people, like the peasant P'ang, on whom a *haiku*, a seventeen-syllable Japanese poem, is said to have been based: 'How wonderful, how miraculous! I fetch wood, I carry water'. His actual words are recorded as: 'Spirit-like understanding and divine functioning *lies* in carrying water and chopping wood.'

In this, as in many other things, there are similarities between Ch'an and earlier Taoism. The *Tao* sage, also, was very much of this world. He practised trance meditation and he expected his disciples to learn by intuition from him through wordless teachings and occasional sudden attacks. Furthermore, the image of the dusty mirror, invoked by Shen-hsiu and Hui-neng, occurs a thousand years earlier in Lao Tse and Chuang Tsu. There is also in Ch'an much of the *Tao*'s sometimes grotesque irreverence and humour, something hitherto unknown in Buddhism. For example, a particular Ch'an master simply burned a wooden statue of the Buddha when he was cold, arguing that it was only a piece of wood, after all, not a relic. Another master announced that Buddha ought to be killed if he ever got in the way – he was merely another form of attachment. Yet another, when asked 'What is the Buddha?' was given to replying 'What is not the Buddha?', 'I never knew him' or 'Wait until there *is* one, then I'll tell you'. In Ch'an, just as in *Tao*, there is little talk of enlightenment as an escape from the world. For fully engaging in life is the path to immortality. In the words of another Ch'an master: 'Only do ordinary things with no special effort: relieve your bowels, pass water, wear your clothes, eat your food and, when tired, lie down! Simple fellows will laugh at you, but the wise will understand.'

Perhaps because of this resonance with the very Chineseness of Taoism – and because Ch'an monks and nuns were willing to work – Ch'an, along with the Pure Land school, survived the ninth-century dissolution of the monasteries relatively unscathed. Five different sub-schools began to appear at around that time, with different styles of teaching and meditational practice. But only two of them were to last – the Tsao-tung (Japanese: Soto) and the Lin-Chi (Japanese: Rinzai) schools. The Tsao-tung school favoured sitting in silent meditation and its founder proposed five steps towards ultimate awareness, based on the Chinese Book of Changes. The Lin-Chi school rejected this kind of meditation (and the study of the *Sutras*) as a way of simply hiding from the world. It was vehemently anti-rationalist; it continued to use the disruptive methods of shout and stick; and it awarded virtually mantric status to the use of meditation on a chosen *kung-an* as an opener of the door to awareness. One of its masters told his students: 'Just steadily go on with your *kung-an* every moment of your life! Whether walking or sitting, let your attention be fixed on it without interruption. When you begin to find it entirely devoid of flavour, the final moment is approaching: do not let it slip out of your grasp! When all of a sudden something flashes out in your mind, its light will illuminate the entire universe.'

Illuminate or no, the *kung-an* tradition – as is clear from these words – somewhere along the way lost its intense creativity. It was no longer a kind of tailor-made spiritual ad-libbing. It had come to rely on set texts. From the beginning of the Sung dynasty (960–1279), this kind of standardization and the ossification of old methods set in all over the *Sangha*. There was also a rise in neo-Confucianism, which was by now equipped with a sophisticated new metaphysic, much of it borrowed from Ch'an. Because of what came to be called 'the persecution', Buddhism had lost its powerful economic base; and with the establishment of a new dynasty and the arrival of peace, the intellectual élite was now more inclined to enter the imperial bureaucracy, where Confucianism ruled – as it did in the educational system – than they were to enter a monastery.

Buddhism in general, therefore, lost its intellectual edge; and because there was no longer any meaningful contact with India and Tibet, due to Muslim invasions, there was no fresh fertilization from outside of either theory or practice. Instead, the different schools began, in effect, to grow together. Some Ch'an practitioners, like the Pure Land societies, took to chanting the name of Amidharba. Pure Land societies awarded the status of a *kung-an* to this chanting and Confucianism absorbed the Tsao-tung practice of quiet meditation into their own 'quiet-sitting' (ching-tso). At the same time, the Buddhist *Sangha* lost prestige because it was controlled by the state and, having no central authority (like a pope and cardinals), could be easily kept in line. This control involved periodic confiscations of wealth and land and forced defrockings of monks and nuns. But it also involved the state selling off certificates of ordination, when times were hard, to whoever could pay the price – even criminals on the run from justice. It is hard not to see the transfiguration of the Buddha-to-Be Maitreya into the so-called 'Hemp-Sack Monk', which happened at this time, as almost an enshrinement of this loss of status. For Pu-tai, known also as the 'Laughing Buddha', is on the face of it a cheeky pot-bellied hedonist – hardly a celebration of spiritual or other-wordly values.

For all this, the Sung period was in many ways a golden age for the Ch'an school. It had a profound influence on cultural life and the arts, particularly on painting. (Many Ch'an monks were among the painters of the period and the simplicity, naturalness and spontaneity of Chinese watercolour and some forms of calligraphy can be said to represent a Ch'an ideal.) Ch'an was also much favoured at court, and many new monasteries were built, which subsequently became important social and cultural centres. In the process, though, Ch'an became more worldly and, in Buddhic terms, infected by impermanence. All over the Sangha, in fact, the period of decline and decadence which Sakamuni had predicted as invevitably stemming from initial creativity, set in. There was a revival under the Ming dynasty, but the only effect in the long run was that the two most original and lasting expressions of Chinese Buddhism, Pure Land and Ch'an, became one. The only hint of revolutionary thinking now came from secret messianic societies that claimed Buddhist connections and took Buddhist names – from which stems the legend of the so-called *kung-fu* monks.

Under the Manchu dynasty, just as with the Ming, Buddhism was tolerated. However, state patronage was given to a rigid form of neo-Confucianism which constantly propagandized against all forms of the faith. Then, in the mid-nineteenth century, when the Chinese empire began to unravel, the T'ai-p'ing rebellion (1850–1864) virtually destroyed Buddhism's monastic base. The rebels, who professed a sort of Christianity, sacked sixteen provinces, destroyed 600 cities and burned thousands of temples and monasteries to the ground. A range of Buddhist organizations were set up in response – Buddhist schools were founded and attempts were made to promote a world fellowship of Buddhists. With the final collapse of the Manchu dynasty, and the arrival of a nationalist government, there was a brief period of relative religious freedom. In 1930 there were still said to be in China 738,000 Buddhist monks and nuns and 267,000 temples.

When the Communists took over the mainland in 1949, though, the Buddhist clergy were quickly denounced as parasites. Their land was confiscated and they were either forced back into secular life or imprisoned and/or brainwashed. The *Sangha* was soon put under the aegis of a Chinese Buddhist Association, which was controlled – like the Orthodox Church in Russia – by the Communist secret police. During the Great Cultural Revolution (1965–1975) that followed, Red Guards went on the rampage and destroyed thousands of surviving Buddhist buildings and monuments, along with all the relics of China's past that they could get their hands on. Now, with the coming of runaway capitalism to China, the omens for Chinese Buddhism continue to look poor.

Chinese Buddhism Abroad

Vietnam and Korea

The same is true for what were once Chinese dependencies: Vietnam and Korea. The northern part of what we now call Vietnam was, for centuries, a province of the Chinese empire. It was also where the Vietnamese people arose, before sweeping south to occupy the whole region. Much earlier, Indian settlers had brought a form of *Theravada* with them to the south, which still survives on the Cambodian border; and this seems to have been followed by the sort of Shiva-Buddhism found in Indonesia. Eventually, though, it was the Ch'an school, which had arrived in the north in the sixth century, that came to dominate the entire country. (Northern Ch'an is unique in that its twenty-eighth patriarch was a Ch'an nun.) Later, a version of Pure Land became popular at village level and, as in China, the distinction between Pure Land and Ch'an began to disappear – though Ch'an remained a powerful influence on the way in which Vietnamese culture developed. In fact, Buddhism remained more or less central to Vietnamese life until French colonialists brought in Roman Catholic missionaries and western-style education. The Vietnam War, the American-backed puppet governments of south Vietnam, and the ultimately victorious Communists of the north did the rest. Between them they managed to undermine and damage the Vietnamese *Sangha* irreparably.

As for Korea, Buddhism seems to have arrived in what were then the Three Kingdoms sometime in the fourth century AD – after which it gradually spread throughout the whole peninsula. By the sixth century it was well enough established to be able to send missionaries to Japan, along with Buddhist statues and texts. The main early schools in Korea were similar to those in China, but when Buddhism was made the state religion in the seventh century the appearance of Ch'an, with its volatile mix of simplicity and iconoclasm, gave them new competition and life. There followed a golden period for Buddhism in Korea, in which members of the royal family often became monks and nuns, and huge sums were spent on building, publishing projects, art and elaborate ceremonies. Buddhist *bonzes*, most of them Ch'an (Korean: Son), controlled the government for long periods of time and Buddhism was rapturously taken up by the common people, who brought to it the sort of magic practices – divination, rain-making, the raising of spirits, etc. – that it had acquired elsewhere.

At the end of the fourteenth century, though, Buddhism in Korea also went into a rapid decline. A new dynasty, the Yi, took power and it favoured, not Buddhism, but the sort of orthodox Confucianism that had taken hold in China under the Ming. Buddhism was eventually disestablished, its land confiscated and its monasteries and convents closed. It survived away from the cities to some extent, and when the Japanese took control of the country (1910–1945), there was a modest revival which saw Buddhism finally united into a single sect. After the defeat of the Japanese, however, land reform took away much of the *Sangha*'s income and although this was soon replaced with state grants in the south, in the north it dealt Buddhism a mortal blow. In today's South Korea Buddhists remain active. But in the North –as in Vietnam and China – land reform, the War and ultimate Communist control have put paid to any fresh revival.

Japan

When Buddhism arrived in Japan in the sixth century AD – by means of missionaries from Korea – the country was in the process of creating a central state out of loose federations of clans. At first it was permitted a grudging toehold, but as more Korean monks began to appear it started to be seen not only as the representative of a higher civilization but also as the guardian of occult powers, through which it could protect against disease and bring good luck and social harmony. Buddhism was soon adopted therefore, by the emerging empire, as an instrument of state, rather than as a bringer of individual salvation.

During the seventh century, temples and monasteries were built under the aegis of a series of devout emperors. Monks were ordained and ceremonies were funded out of the public purse. Buddhism proved adept at assimilating the deities or spirits (*kami*) of indigenous Shinto; and it soon became, in effect, the official Religion and Civilization Department of the imperial court. Tradition has it that the Empress Suiko became a devout Buddhist nun and that her nephew, Prince Shotuku, who lectured on the *Sutras* himself, wrote the first 'constitution' of the country under the direction of Buddhist monks. He is still known as the founder of Japanese Buddhism.

The faith was no doubt helped in Japan by the fact that Confucianists made poor missionaries: they did not like to travel or proselytize among 'barbarians'. But, for whatever reason, Buddhism became the main conduit for the wholesale importation into Japan of Chinese architecture, technology and literary and artistic forms. Buddhism may have largely been the preferred religion of the intellectual élite – at least at first – but it helped shape the culture of the entire country. (It is said that the only original cultural or technological artefact that Japan exported back to mainland China was the folding fan.)

In time, ordained Japanese monks went on pilgrimage to China, and the early Buddhist sects that appeared in Japan seem to have depended on who their teachers were. Groups of monks – largely gentlemen-scholars – gathered around particular texts and only one of the groups (*Hosso*, based on *Fa-hsiang* teachings) survived to become a fully-developed school. It wasn't in fact until the time of the building of the capital at Nara in the eighth century that a Chinese philosophical system rose to any prominence. This was the Hua-yen school, known as Kegon in Japan, which equated the emperor with the Celestial Buddha Vairocana and Japanese society as a whole with the Hua-yen *Dharma*-realm, in which everything interpenetrated everything else via a seamless web of connection. This vision of the Japanese world that was created by and centred on the emperor/Buddha proved so effective in making the link between individuals and their collective fealty to the state that a colossal bronze image of Vairocana was erected in Nara's Eastern Great Temple in 752, where it remains today.

In general, though, the doctrines promoted by the different schools were less important than the generic state Buddhism that was set up in the provinces by imperial edict and the lasting effect on Japanese culture that it had. Knowledge of Chinese spread through translation of the *Sutras,* and the making of cult objects stimulated virtually every art and craft, from sculpture to papermaking. Monks introduced geomancy, astronomy and calendars to the country. They not only served as scribes and clerks in the developing Japanese bureaucracy but also as engineers: building irrigation systems, bridges and roads. They encouraged public bathing and cremation, as in China, and even made the first maps. So powerful did the Nara monks become that at the end of the seventh century the capital was shifted to Heia (now Kyoto) to rusticate them. From then on the focus of Buddhism shifted from metropolitan centres to monastery-settlements in the mountains.

Monasteries in the Mountains

One of these monastery-powerhouses was on Mount Hiei, northwest of Kyoto, which became the main centre for a *Tantra*-influenced form of the Chinese T'ien-t'ai school (known as Tendai). This had been brought to Japan by a Japanese monk called Saicho or Dengyo-daishi ('Great Master Who Transmitted the Teaching'), who kept his monks in mountain seclusion while they underwent a rigorous twelve-year course of study and meditation. At its height, the temple complex of the Mount Hiei community contained 3,000 buildings – among them halls set aside for the Pure-Land chanting of Amidhaba's name (*Amida*) and fully 30,000 monks. From its ranks came the founders of almost all the new schools which followed in later centuries.

Another powerful centre was the monastery settlement on

Mount Koya, which became the headquarters of the Japanese version of the Mantra or Tantric School, Shingon (Chinese: *Chen-yen*, 'Truth-Word'). Shingon, with its emphasis on *mantras, mudras, mandalas* and contemplation, was brought to Japan by an aristocratic monk called Kukai or Kobo-daishi ('Great Master Who Propagated the *Dharma*'), who was much favoured by the imperial court for his occult powers and skill in rain-making. Kukai was also a prolific writer and sculptor, an educationalist, a promoter of the arts and a skilled calligrapher – he is said to have invented the cursive syllabary of forty-seven signs in which, with the sometime addition of Chinese characters, the language is written and he remains perhaps the most celebrated scholar-teacher in Japanese history. Under his rule, disciples flocked to Mount Koya for instruction and many of them followed the path of the early ascetics, living alone or in groups in the forests (as they also did on Mount Hiei). Followers of Shingon still maintain that Kukai is not dead, but is merely waiting on Mount Koya to rise up again with the coming into the world of the Buddha-to-be, Maitreya.

During the so-called Heian period (794–1184), there seems to have been considerable cross-fertilization between these and other sects. Tendai, for example, took over much of Shingon's esotericism; Shingon adopted Tendai Amidist invocations; and the Nara and the mountain monks not only came to set great store on the arts but also on elaborate rituals, chanting and ceremony (the ground-base for the later emergence of Noh drama.) But there was also intense competition both between the sects and between individual monasteries. Armies of mercenaries led by warrior monks (*sohei*) regularly attacked and burned down rival institutions. From time to time they even invaded the capital to assert their political will.

Often paid a kind of tribute money (or rental on the faith) by their provincial offshoots, the monastic institutions had become major centres of wealth and power by the end of the Heian period. The monks were still largely drawn from the élite: many of them were aristocrats and therefore no strangers either to earthly pride or the arts of war. Towards the end of the era, Amidism, with its *Nembutsu* (*Namu-Amida-butsu*) chant, began to spread among ordinary people, but for the most part Heian Buddhism remained a very exclusive affair.

In the era that followed, the so-called Kamakura period (1185–1333), this was to change for ever. For it was a period of crisis, when Japan was threatened by Mongolian invasion and disrupted at the same time by internal disunity, marked by a shift in power between the capital and the provinces. A disaffected new class had appeared, that's to say, made up of *samurai* (warriors) and provincial landowners, and although it was nominally Buddhist it was reluctant to support either an esoteric faith or an emperor in some distant capital. The result was the establishment of a new centre of power in Kamakura in 1185, in the form of a Shogunate (or military government), and a new democratization of Japanese Buddhism. For the new class, which needed popular support, succeeded in bridging the yawning gap that had existed between the old aristocracy and the peasantry. High Japanese culture was diffused across every class in the country; and Buddhism in the process became a distinctively Japanese coloration for the first time.

New Sects and Schools

Times of anxiety and violent change do not generally favour the pursuit of abstruse philosophy or the systematic deferment of gratification; and both the laity and a number of Buddhist monks seem to have felt this equally. For following the lead of early Amidist missionaries, two new popular devotional schools were quickly established by disaffected monks schooled at Mount Hiei. The first was Jodo-shu ('Pure Land'), founded by a learned Tendai monk called Honen (1133–1212), who had become convinced that enlightenment, given the nature of the times, could no longer be reached through personal effort (*jiriki*) alone. It now required the supernatural intercession of Amida, whose name had to be ceaselessly invoked through the *Nembutsu*. Honen preached that even the greatest sinner could be reborn in the Western Paradise by this means, so long as he had faith, avoided sin and not only paid due respect not only to Amida but also to the other Buddhas and the *Sutras*. Pure-Land Buddhism soon found favour with both court and commoner, and it still exists as a school today, although a later modification of its central teaching proclaimed that rebirth in the Pure Land involved a change of mind and condition rather than translation to another cosmic region.

The second school, founded by ex-Tendai monk Shinran (1173–1262), was Jodo Shinsu, or 'True Pure Land' which threw the net of Amidism even wider. No personal effort at all was either needed or recommended in Jodo Shinsu. All that was necessary was to take up Amida's gift in a state of faith, and after that the fate of the individual lay in the Buddha's beneficent hands. Shinran abandoned monastic rule and married a young aristocrat, as if to demonstrate that living in the everyday world was as redeemable a condition as any other. Indeed, he argued that as he had become a sinner he was more likely to gain access to the Western Paradise, because he had given up self-help and the path of merit and had literally nowhere else to turn. His teachings made salvation easily accessible to ordinary people, among whom he spent the rest of his life – and he remains much revered today.

A third devotional sect, with a difference, was founded by yet another monk from Mount Hiei, Nichiren Shonin (1222–1282). The son of a humble fisherman, Nichiren had become as frustrated as Honen and Shinran with the ineffectiveness of the monastic regime, but he chose a different path. He maintained that the *Lotus Sutra* was the essential and pure *summa* of Buddhism and that men and women could achieve the Enlightenment of Sakyamuni Buddha by merely invoking it with the words *Namu-myoho-renge-kyo* ('Homage to the Lotus Sutra'). Enlightenment was not deferred as in Pure Land, but obtainable right now – they would become embodiments of paradise. Not to take this step, he preached, would be to deny the whole country its manifest destiny as an earthly and inviolable Buddha-land, from which the *Dharma* – and all things Japanese – would go out to conquer the world. It meant that apocalypse – at first in the shape of a Mongol invasion – would surely come.

Nichiren's role, as he saw it, was to cure the country of its social and political disorders by uniting it under the banner of the *Lotus Sutra* and rooting out all the other schools which had led to the poisoning of the Japanese state and soul. He denounced Shingon and the Amidist schools for worshipping Vairocana and Amida rather than the Sakyamuni Buddha and Zen for paying attention to the historical Buddha rather than the eternal Buddha of the *Sutra*. He was a zealot, uncompromising and virulent. '*Nembutsu* is hell', he said, 'the Zen are devils; Shingon is a national ruin; and the Risshu are traitors to the country.' He was twice exiled for these views, but persecution only made him more messianic. Conze says of him drily: 'On this occasion [i.e. in the figure of Nichiren] Buddhism had evolved its very antithesis out of itself.' Neverthless Nichiren came to be widely admired for his stubborn grit and – when Mongol fleets did invade (only to be beaten back) – for his gifts as a prophet. His brand of nationalistic Buddhism, if that is what it is, remains highly influential today.

Zen

The most important of the schools that Nichiren attacked – and more important to Japanese history, in the end, than any of the devotional schools, including his own – was Zen (Chinese: Ch'an) which had probably been brought to Japan in the seventh century, but did not become popular until the beginning of the Kamukara period, when it emerged as the most significant alternative to the populism of the devotional cults.

Devotees of Zen believed that although the times might be difficult and degenerate, Enlightenment was still open to those who dared to concentrate every personal resource available on its attainment. Stripped of all ritual and doctrinal study, Zen was down to earth and practical and it stressed exactly what the devotional sects denied: self-power. For this reason, it appealed greatly to the *samurai*, who constantly lived under the shadow of death and needed to see the way they lived, not as a dead end but as something they could control as part of a general spiritual development. Thus Buddhism, in its Zen form, contributed hugely to *Bushido*, the 'Way of the Warrior', for it enabled the *samurai* to confront death calmly and it transformed their skills into adaptations of Buddhist ritual and contemplation: true martial arts such as Zen archery, judo and kendo. The goal in these arts, in the words of Robinson and Johnson:

> is to realize a perfect fusion of aesthetic perception and noumenal awareness, of stillness and motion, utility and grace, conformity and spontaneity.

By invoking a form of action beyond thought, the Zen *samurai* could learn to act, even in war, in perfect harmony with the spirit of the moment and escape from concern for his own personal safety into another (and impersonal) realm.

There are two main surviving schools in the Japanese version of Chinese Ch'an – the Lin-chi and the T'sao-tung, known as Rinzai and Soto respectively. Rinzai was brought to Japan in the late twelfth century by a monk called Eisai (1141–1215) who, after running foul of Tendai influence at the Kyoto court, eventually set up his first temple in Kamakura and forged the alliance with the warrior class that became Zen's most important social foundation. He also wrote a nationalist tract called *Propagate Zen, Protect the Country*. Soto, which is in general more quietist – hence the expression 'Rinzai is for the general; Soto is for the farmer' – was founded by Dogen (1200–1253), who may first have studied Zen under Eisai's successor. An aristocrat who had became a monk at thirteen after being orphaned, he subsequently spent four years in China, and on his return, like Eisai, he turned his back on the capital and settled in a small rural temple in an eastern province. But he attracted so many disciples there – who had perhaps read his chief work, *The Eye of the True Law*, written in Japanese – that he had to move several times. He finally settled in a mountain temple, Eihei-ji, not far from Kamakura, which remains one of the two most important centres of his school today.

The difference between Rinzai and Soto was, and remains, largely one of emphasis. Both maintained the importance of *zazen* ('sitting-cross-legged meditation') as a pure religious exercise, although in Soto, which incorporated the belief that man was already enlightened from birth, to be in *zazen* was actually to be in the enlightened state, giving thanks to the Buddha. *Zazen* in Rinzai was much more purposive; and in general the school was more militant and aggressive, continuing to make use of the shout-and-stick approach and the *koan* (the Chinese *kung-an*). Rinzai, furthermore, rejected the study of the *Sutras* as useless, but was tolerant of worldly ambition, while Soto tended to encourage book-learning and preached abandonment of fame and fortune. Today, even these differences, never great, have by and large been eroded. In the words of Wilson Ross in *his Hinduism, Buddhism, Zen*:

> In the Rinzai sect we find the dynamic character of the daring koan experiment and of lightning-like enlightenment, while the Soto School is characterised by a preference for silent sitting in zazen and the quiet deeds of everyday life. It appears [however] . . . that adherence to one sect or the other is determined largely by the spiritual bent of the monks, who are inherently suited to one tradition or the other and pursue enlightenment in a way appropriate to their character. Thus one can find in the temples of the Soto sect men of brilliant wit and dynamic character who devote themelves to the koan exercises, while on the other hand certain Rinzai monks of subdued character can scarcely be distinguished from Soto disciples.

The differences, then, between the two Zen Schools should perhaps not be stressed too much. What cannot be overemphasized, however, is the contribution that they made between them to Japanese culture. At the end of the Kamakura period, and through the age of the Ashikaga Shoguns (1335–1573) that followed, Zen monks produced huge numbers of texts in Japanese; they opened schools, devised new methods of accounting and conducted widespread trade with China. Much more importantly, however, Zen doctrine itself – with its emphasis on concrete action rather than speculative thought – came to permeate almost every aspect of the national character. A Zen-derived code of behaviour took hold, as described by Edward Conze:

Actions must be simple, and yet have depth – and 'simple elegance' (wabi or sabi) became the accepted ideal of conduct.

Wabi (or *sabi*) was a central principle carried over through Zen into every form of human expression. It was exemplified in the tea ceremony (*cha-no yu*) that was systematized by Zen masters in the sixteenth century. (Tea was said to have been first brought to Japan by Ch'an masters as an aid to meditation.) But it found expression too, in garden and house design, calligraphy, ink painting, sculpture, pottery, music, Noh theatre and even the art of flower-arranging (*ikebana*). All these arts, at their core, are imbued with a profoundly Buddhist sentiment that combines the awareness of transiency, aloneness (no-self), compassion for living things and an understanding that the Buddha-nature is everywhere in the here and now – Enlightenment and the mundane natural world are one. This sentiment finds its best expression, perhaps, in the seventeen-syllable *haiku*, some of which were written as 'farewell songs' by Zen masters facing death:

> Fifty-three years
> This clumsy ox has managed,
> Now barefoot stalks
> The Void – What nonsense!

> Life's as we
> Find it – death too
> A parting poem?
> Why insist?

Perhaps the most famous of all *haikus*, however, was written by a Zen layman, Japan's greatest poet, Matsuo Basho, in the seventeenth century:

On this road
With no traveller
Autumn night falls.

Autumn night did fall, in a sense, on Japanese Buddhism at the end of the Ashikaga period. For a warlord named Nobunaga (1534–1582) ruthlessly set about the pacification and reunification of Japan – and for this the great monasteries, being independent and often fortified centres of power, had to be destroyed. He razed the temples and libraries on Mount Hiei to the ground, slaughtering most of its 20,000 monks; and his successor Hyegashi did the same to the Shingon headquarters at Negoro. Zen, which had never fortified its monasteries, survived – many of its temples can still be seen in Kyoto. But when unification was finally achieved in 1603 – and the Tokugawa Shogunate was set up at Edo (modern Tokyo) – it too paid a heavy price. For the Shogunate, which ruled Japan for over 250 years, closed the country to foreigners and imposed an internal authoritarian régime which stifled all innovation. New teachings and practices were simply forbidden, as was the opening of new temples and schools. Doctrinal disputes were decided by the state, which favoured rigid orthodoxy, not to mention an austere and feudal Confucianism. At the same time, in order to combat the spread of Christianity, the entire population was required to register at an existing temple with the result that Buddhism was increasingly seen as merely the religious arm of the central power.

There were, for all this a few bright spots. A new form of simplified Zen called Obaka arrived from China through the open port of Nagasaki, along with new Chinese styles of ritual, architecture and clothing. A number of inspirational figures also appeared on the home front, among them Hakuin Zenji (1685–1768), a much-revered monk who reformed Rinzai Zen, restored the use of *koan* and laid down the template for the development of Zen down to the present day. It was Hakuin who coined the famous koan of 'The Sound of One Hand Clapping,' described by Paul Reps in his book *Zen Flesh, Zen Bones*, although used, perhaps as a set text, by another master:

> The master of Kennin Temple was Mokurai, Silent Thunder. He had a little protegé named Toyo who was only twelve years old. Toyo saw the older disciples visit the master's room each morning and evening to receive instructions in sanzen, or personal guidance, in which they were given koans to stop mind-wandering.
>
> Toyo wished to do sanzen also. 'Wait a while' said Mokurai. 'You are too young'.
>
> But the child insisted, so the teacher finally consented.
>
> In the evening little Toyo went at the proper time to the threshold of Mokurai's sanzen room. He struck the gong to announce his presence, bowed respectfully three times outside the door, and went to sit before the master in respectful silence.
>
> 'You can hear the sound of two hands when they clap together', said Mokurai. 'Now show me the sound of one hand'.
>
> Toyo bowed and went to his room to consider this problem. From his window he could hear the music of the geishas. 'Ah, I have it!' he proclaimed.

The next evening, when his teacher asked him to illustrate the sound of one hand, Toyo began to play the music of the geishas.

'No. no', said Mokurai. 'That will never do. That is not the sound of one hand. You've not got it at all'.

Thinking that such music might interrupt, Toyo moved his abode to a quiet place. He meditated again. 'What can the sound of one hand be?' He happened to hear some water dripping. 'I have it', imagined Toyo.

When he next appeared before his teacher, Toyo imitated dripping water.

'What is that?' asked Mokurai. 'That is the sound of dripping water, but not the sound of one hand. Try again'.

In vain Toyo meditated to hear the sound of one hand. He heard the sighing of the wind. But the sound was rejected. He heard the cry of an owl. This was also refused. The sound of one hand was not the locusts.

For more than ten times Toyo visited Mokurai with different sounds. All were wrong. For almost a year he pondered what the sound of one hand might be.

At last little Toyo entered true meditation and transcended all sounds. 'I could collect no more', he explained later, 'so I reached the soundless sound'.

Toyo had realized the sound of one hand.

Buddhism's Struggle for Survival

In 1868 – partly under pressure from the West and partly inspired by a Shinto nationalism hostile to Buddhism – a coup-d'état finally restored the imperial régime. Shinto became the state religion, the Meiji Emperor was given the status of a god, and Buddhism was disendowed – its land expropriated and its temples either closed or destroyed. Paradoxically, however, this seemed to give the faith a new lease of life, for Buddhist schools and universities were established once the persecution had diminished and contacts were made with other Buddhist countries and with the West. New editions of Pali, Sanskrit, Tibetan and Chinese texts were produced.

Buddhism retained its popularity among ordinary people, meanwhile – although in the 1920s and 1930s it was Nichiren, with its nationalist message of Japan as a promised Buddha-land destined to spread the *Dharma* abroad, that came to the fore. Though almost all Buddhist schools acquiesced in the Japanese conquests of Manchuria and Korea and condoned Japan's entry into World War II, it was Nichiren that set the brutal overall tone.

After the War, the American occupying forces' 'land reforms' brought financial ruin to the monasteries and led to a widespread revival of Nichiren among the laity. Perhaps forty per cent of all those who call themselves Buddhists in Japan today are members of Rissho Kosei-kai and Soka Gakkai, two of the many so-called 'New Religions' – both of them lay offshoots of Nichiren. In some ways they resemble American organizations like the Kiwanis or the Shriners, in that they offer practical support for their members and stress both wordly success and involvement with social issues. (They are also very careful to stress that their ultimate aim is world peace.) Conze says of them somewhat drily:

This is one of Buddhism's more successful attempts to come to terms with the 'American Century'. One may well doubt whether capitalism has been any more kind to the Buddhists than communism.

In the meantime, the traditional schools have still managed to preserve an impressive roster of temples, clergy and lay followers, for they too have regenerated themselves, to a degree, in response to the modern world. (Jodo-shu and Jodo Shinsu, for example, still have considerable followings.) Serious meditation, however, has on the whole become neglected. Zen meditation halls, though open to the laity, are ill attended – which may explain why so many Zen *roshi*, particularly, have come to the West in search of fallower ground, following in the footsteps of the first able interpreter of Zen in the West, Dr. D.T. Suzuki.

Afterword:

The Present

There is a melancholy note that has sounded out from within Buddhism, almost from its beginnings. This plangency is variously expressed: 'Everything is impermanent, even the power of the Buddha's example'; 'We live in a degenerate age in which self-effort is no longer enough to achieve awareness'; and, especially, 'The Buddha's teachings will lose their efficacy after two-and-a-half thousand years and it will take many thousands more before the Buddha-to-Be, Maitreya, appears in the world to renew them . . .'

The 2,500th anniversary of the Sakyamuni Buddha was, in fact, celebrated in India in the 1950s; and shortly thereafter the young Dalai Lama fled from Tibet, as a Chinese army set about ruthlessly destroying every last trace of *Vajrayana* Buddhism. The earlier pessimism suddenly seemed to be completely justified; the prediction was fully accurate. Everywhere the light of the *Dharma* was being extinguished. The shamanic Buddhism of Outer Mongolia had already been destroyed by Soviet Communism. In China, Buddhism had been denounced as parasitic and its monks and nuns had been defrocked or imprisoned or worse. In Japan, the faith had been undermined by American occupation and popular forms of Buddhism were emerging which bypassed the whole monastic tradition, and were only really Buddhist in name.

Worse was yet to come. Following the path of North Korea, Buddhism was virtually eliminated in Vietnam, Laos and Cambodia, the victim, in equal parts, of two branches of materialism: American capitalism-in-arms and Marxist-Leninism. Burma fell to a heavy-handed dictatorship. In Thailand, Buddhist monks were co-opted into an anti-communist campaign – some were even seen blessing American tanks. The only bright spot seemed to be the conversion to Buddhism of huge numbers of lowest-caste Indian 'Untouchables' – called by Mahatma Gandhi the *Harijan*, or 'Children of God' – although that had largely been a political decision, taken by their leaders.

There is no inherent reason for the endurance of any religion. Mithraism and Manichaeanism – extremely powerful in their day – both disappeared, after all. Christianity vanished from its Eastern heartland under Muslim occupation and, in this century, Confucianism has ceased to be a religion. It is always possible for the book to be closed and for us to say: 'Ah yes, Buddhism – a very beautiful religion indeed. A doctrine of salvation even older than Christianity, yet completely unmarked by violence, religious wars, inquisitions, crusades or the burning of witches. It flourished in some of the most remarkable periods in human history and it left behind it astonishing buildings and works of art, a vast literature and an extremely sophisticated and dense metaphysics – which we no longer understand.'

And yet Buddhism has proved itself remarkably adaptable over its (now) more than 2,500 years. From *Sutras* to *Hinayana* to *Mahayana* to *Tantra* to *Zen*, it has consistently found ways to accommodate a new environment or altered social conditions, without losing sight of its central aim of Enlightenment, or the road to it via

230

compassion. It continues to maintain: 'Right beliefs, right knowledge, right conduct' – a central message with which few could argue. Also, being a doctrine without a creator god, it continues to be extremely tolerant of other forms of worship.

It is true that Buddhism has so far been ill-equipped to withstand the inroads of materialism and scientific rationalism (from which Christianity, too, has taken a bludgeoning). Its traditions of pacifism and acceptance have precluded any fighting back. Yet in the past it has taken five or six hundred years for it to emerge each time in a new accommodative form – so by that reckoning another of its creative transformations is soon due. One prophecy has it that after being played out in the East it will appear once more, newly energized, in 'the land of the red-faced people' – which many have assumed to mean the West. And indeed there are signs that more and more urbanists and professionals in the West, dissatisfied with the loss of the magical and spiritual in their lives, are already turning to Buddhism – just as the early town-dwellers in India did during the Sakyamuni Buddha's earthly mission.

So far the Western approach to Buddhism has been fairly haphazard and scattergun. Individuals have tended to cherry-pick for what suits them in available schools, without approaching the central mystery of awareness in any disciplined way. Buddhist monks and adepts living in the West as exiles from their native countries have equally - with some notable exceptions like Dr. Suzuki - found it difficult to adapt the Buddhist message, and themselves, to Western life. But the ground has already been laid. For Western philosophers from Schopenhauer onwards – and psychologists like Jung – have found important resonances for their ideas within Buddhism. Physicists, too, like Fritjof Kapra, have begun to mine Buddhist metaphysics for its understanding of the nature of reality. Many of the central texts have been translated, just as they were in China before the characteristic forms of Chinese Buddhism appeared. Westerners have travelled east to study in monasteries, as the founders of the Japanese schools did in China. Buddhist missionaries have appeared in the West, as they did once in Central Asia and Tibet. Comparative scholars have done their work. All that remains, perhaps, is for time to pass, time that will allow for consolidation and for a fresh – and perhaps characteristically Western – pathway to Enlightenment to unfold.

Bibliography

Batchelor, Stephen, *The Jewel in the Lotus: A Guide to the Buddhist Traditions of Tibet*, Wisdom Publications, 1987.

Carus, Paul, *The Gospels of Buddha*, Oneworld, 1994.

Connolly, Holly and Peter, *Buddhism*, Stanley Thones, 1992.

Conze, Edward, Buddhism: *Its Essence and Development*, Cassirer, 1960.

Conze, Edward, *A Short History of Buddhism*, Oneworld, 1993.

Erricker, Clive, *Buddhism*, Hodder and Stoughton, 1995.

Gelsin, Rupert, *The Foundations of Buddhism*, Oxford University Press, 1998

Hope, Jane and Van Loon, Borin, *Buddha For Beginners*, Icon Books, 1994.

Humphreys, Christopher, *A Popular Dictionary of Buddhism*, Curzon Press, 1975.

Ikeda, Daisaku, *The Living Buddha*, Weatherhill, 1995.

Ling, Trevor, *The Buddha*, Penguin Books, 1973.

Pagels, Elaine, *The Gnostic Gospels*, Weidenfeld & Nicholson, 1979.

Palmer, Martin, *Elements of Taoism*, Element Books, 1991.

Rahula, Walpola, *What the Buddha Taught*, Wisdom Books, 1985.

Reps, Paul, *Zen Flesh, Zen Bones*, Pelican Books, 1972.

Robinson, Richard H. and Johnson, Willard L., *The Buddhist Religion, A Historical Introduction*, Wadsworth Publishing, Third Edition, 1982.

Scott, David and Doubleday, Tony, *Elements of Zen*, Element Books, 1992.

Snelling, John, *The Buddhist Handbook: A Complete Guide to Buddhist Teaching and Practice*, Century Hutchinson, 1987.

Snelling, John, *Elements of Buddhism*, Element Books, 1990.

Stokes, Gillian, *Buddha: A Beginner's Guide*, Hodder & Stoughton Educational, 2000.

Thomas, Edward J., *The Life of the Buddha*, Kegan Paul, 1949.

Watts, Alan, *The Way of Zen*, Penguin Books, 1962.

Index

Index

Index

Index

mind 63, 73, 140

missionaries 115, 116

monasteries 46 – 7, 102, 214, 215

monastic rules 45, 91 – 3, 99 – 101

monks and nuns 43 – 7, 90 – 4, 109 – 13, 121

   in China 154 – 5

   in Japan 213 – 19

morality (*sila*) 47, 57 – 8, 68 – 71, 83 – 5, 128

mudras 187

Muslim invasions 189, 208

N

Nagarjuna 139, 140, 155

Name and Form 73

Nepal 143, 189, 190

nirvana 40, 58, 79 – 82, 81 – 2, 105

Nyingma 180 – 2

O

ordination 44, 45, 90 – 1

P

pacceka buddhas 90, 126

Pali canon 25, 109, 117, 123, 162

paranirvana 52, 54

patience (*ksanti*) 128

perception (*skandhas*) 42, 44, 64

Personalists (*Pudgalavadins*) 104 – 6

pre-Buddhist cults 117 – 18

Pure Land School 134, 158, 196 – 8, 207, 211, 217

Q

Questions of King Milinda 115

R

Rahula, son of Buddha 28, 30, 46

Rains Retreats 46

rebirth 19, 22, 36, 66 – 72, 74, 76, 77, 112

restlessness 88

Rig Veda 17

Rinzai 220, 221, 224

ritual objects 168

Rock Edicts 114

roshi (Ch'an master) 198

'royal discipline' (*raja-yoga*) 31 – 2

S

sacred places 117 – 20

sacrificial rituals 21, 22

saddhu (wandering holy man) 30, 163

Saghamitta 121 – 2

saints (*arhants*) 43, 89 – 90, 102 – 3, 111, 124

Sakya 178

Sakyamuni see Buddha

salvation 59, 153

Samantabhadra 131 – 2

Sangharakshita 48

Sanskrit 17

Sanskrit literature 122 – 3, 145, 149

Sayings of the Ancient Worthies 203

schisms 101 – 8

schools of Buddhism 102 – 8, 116 – 17, 122

   in China 194 – 210

   in Japan 212 – 17

Index

Index